GETTING
ITALIAN

Second Edition

COLONNA
MOLTO
VECCHIA

A QUICK BEGINNER'S COURSE FOR TOURISTS AND BUSINESS PEOPLE

Emmanuela Tandello

BARRON'S

In cooperation with BBC Languages

First edition for the United States
published 1996 by Barron's Educational Series, Inc.
in cooperation with BBC Languages
a division of BBC Worldwide Ltd.
Woodlands, 80 Wood Lane, London W12 OTT

A Word to the Reader:
Because exchange rates of foreign currencies against the U.S. dollar vary from day to day, the actual cost of a hotel room, a taxi ride, or a meal may be more or less than the amounts in this book. Please consult a newspaper, bank, or currency house for the most up-to-date exchange rate.

Portions of the reference section of this book from *Italian at a Glance* by Mario Consantino.

All inquiries should be addressed to:
Barron's Educational Series, Inc.
250 Wireless Boulevard
Hauppauge, New York 11788

Library of Congress Catalog Card No. 95-53095

International Standard Book No. 0-8120-8444-6 (book and cassette)
0-8120-9681-9 (book)

Library of Congress Cataloging-in-Publication Data
Tandello, Emmanuela.
  Getting by in Italian : a quick beginner's course for tourists and business people /
Emmanuela Tandello.
    p.   cm.
  Rev. ed. of: Get by in Italian. c1992.
  ISBN 0-8120-8444-6 (book-cassette pkg.). —ISBN 0-8120-9681-9 (book)
  1. Italian language—Textbooks for foreign speakers—English.
I. Tandello, Emmanuela. Get by in Italian.   II. Title.
PC1128.T36 1996
458.2'421—dc20
                                                                          95-53095
                                                                          CIP

Printed in Hong Kong
987654

CONTENTS

INTRODUCTION

Barron's new *Getting by in Italian* is a six unit course for anyone planning a visit to Italy, whether for pleasure or business. It aims to provide the basic language and information for some of the most common situations of a visit abroad.

The course consists of a book and two 90 minute cassettes, to be used *together*. Each unit deals with specific areas of conversation: saying hello, shopping, travelling around, getting somewhere to stay, eating out, meeting people and doing business.

The *Getting by* book includes:
- the key words and phrases for each unit;
- the texts of the recorded dialogues in the order they'll be heard on the cassettes;
- notes on each dialogue and a section at the end of each unit giving explanations of the language met; you will need to refer forward to these explanations in order to do some of the exercises;
- background information worth knowing about Italy and Italian customs;
- self-checking exercises for you to do between dialogues, and at the end of each unit (*Can you get by?*).

   (When you come across the cassette only exercise symbol ☆, listen to your tape for your instructions *and* for your answer, as it will not always appear in the key).

- a short reference section or appendix containing a guide to the basics of Italian pronunciation and extra language notes;
- the keys to the exercises and the transcripts of the listening exercises that you'll hear on the cassettes;
- a word list.

The *Getting by* cassettes contain all the dialogues, help with the language used in them, and listening and speaking exercises. They give you plenty of opportunity to practice all the key words and phrases at your own pace. Words which are introduced on the tape can be found in the Explanations section of the same unit.

To make the most of the course:

- The book and cassettes are designed to be used together. But, of course, you can reinforce what you have learned by re-listening to the cassettes while driving, for example.

- The following symbols stand for book only ☐☐ and cassette only ☆ exercises.

- The cassette exercises and language practice have been devised to allow you as much room for repetition as possible. Pauses are left for you to repeat words and phrases and to give answers in the exercises; but winding back and listening again and repeating improves your mastery of the language – so do so as many times as you feel you want and need to! You will certainly need to listen to the dialogues several times over.

- The dialogues are authentic: they are recordings of real people using real language in real situations. There will be plenty of words you don't understand, just as there will be when you go to Italy. Don't panic! Listen for the words you do know, and try to understand the gist of what is being said from that. Equally, when it comes to speaking, don't worry about making mistakes; the important thing is to make yourself understood. Of course, if you've already learned some Latin, French or Spanish, don't hesitate to guess at the Italian forms; they are usually very similar.

We wish you good luck with your Italian . . . *Buon viaggio!*
. . . *e buon divertimento!*

1 SAYING HELLO & ORDERING DRINKS

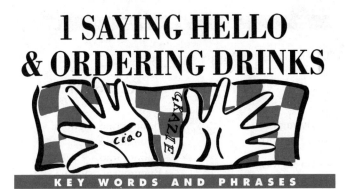

KEY WORDS AND PHRASES

buongiorno	hello, good morning
ciao	hello, hi, 'bye
buonasera	good evening
arrivederci	goodbye
grazie	thank you
prego	don't mention it
sì	yes
no	no
uno, due, tre	1, 2, 3
quattro, cinque	4, 5
sei, sette	6, 7
otto, nove, dieci	8, 9, 10
per favore	please
un caffè	a coffee
un bicchiere di vino	a glass of wine
quant'è?	how much is it?
posso cambiare . . . ?	can I change . . . ?

DIALOGUES

Listen to these exchanges on the cassettes:

SAYING HELLO AND GOODBYE

1

— Buongiorno.
— Buongiorno.

— Buongiorno.
— Buongiorno.
— Buongiorno.

— Buongiorno, signora.
— Buongiorno.

— Buongiorno.
— Buongiorno, signora.

buongiorno (literally good day) is used both to greet people and to say goodbye.
signora (literally madam) is more frequently used than its English equivalent.

2

— Buonasera!
— Buonasera!
— Buonasera!
— Buonasera!

— Buonasera, signori.
— Buonasera.
— Buonasera, dottore.

buonasera good evening, is the usual greeting from mid-afternoon onwards; it is used both to greet people and to say goodbye.
signori gentlemen; gentleman is *signore; signori,* however, is also used for ladies and gentlemen.
dottore doctor, though not necessarily a medical one; a title used for professional people such as engineers, solicitors, etc.

3

— Ciao!
— Ciao!
— Ciao!
— Ciao Isabella!

— Ciao!
— Ciao Sergio!
— Ciao Francesca!

ciao hello, hi! – the informal greeting used with friends and family. It also means goodbye.

4
— Arrivederci!
— Arrivederci!
— Arrivederci!

— Arrivederci!
— Arrivederci, buongiorno.

arrivederci goodbye, is used at any time of day, with anybody, and can be followed by *buongiorno* or *buonasera*.

SAYING THANK YOU
AND DON'T MENTION IT

5
— Grazie.
— Grazie.
— Grazie.
— Grazie, buongiorno.

— Buongiorno, grazie.
— Grazie, buongiorno.
— Buongiorno, grazie, signora.

6
— Grazie.
— Prego.
— Grazie.
— Prego.

— Grazie.
— Prego.
— Grazie.
— Prego.

grazie thank you
prego don't mention it; please is *per favore*

LEARNING TO COUNT

7
— Uno, due, tre, quattro, cinque, sei, sette, otto, nove, dieci.

8
CATERINA   Allora! Uno . . . di' uno . . . di' uno?
                  Uno.

MARIA LUISA	Uno.
CATERINA	Due.
MARIA LUISA	Due.
CATERINA	Tre.
MARIA LUISA	Tre.
CATERINA	Quattro . . . Quattro, prova a dire.
MARIA LUISA	Quattro.
CATERINA	Cinque . . . Di' cinque.
MARIA LUISA	Cinque.
CATERINA	Sei . . . Di' sei.
MARIA LUISA	Sei.
CATERINA	Poi sette.
MARIA LUISA	Sette.
CATERINA	Otto . . . Sai dire otto?
MARIA LUISA	Otto.
CATERINA	Nove.
MARIA LUISA	. . . e dieci.
ADULTI	. . . Nove e dieci!

allora now then
prova a dire try to say
di' . . . say . . .
poi then
sai dire . . . ? can you say . . . ?
e and

Exercise 1 ☆
Listen to Sergio giving his daughter some practice at numbers. See if you can do the sums in Italian! Before you start, two new words: *più* plus, *meno* minus. The answers are in the Key on page 105.

Exercise 2 ☆
Listen to the cassette and try to write down the telephone numbers that are given.
(Transcript on page 105.)

9

FRANCESCA	Puoi cambiarmi diecimila lire?
ISABELLA	Sì certo. Mille, duemila, tremila, quattromila, cinquemila, seimila, settemila, ottomila, novemila, diecimila.
FRANCESCA	Grazie mille.
ISABELLA	Prego.

puoi cambiarmi . . . ? can you change . . . . for me?
certo certainly
grazie mille thanks (literally a thousand thanks)

10

SERGIO	Vuole qualcosa da bere? Abbiamo limonata, aranciata, caffè, coca-cola, tè e acqua minerale.

vuole . . . ? would you like . . . ?
qualcosa da bere something to drink; you can adapt this phrase to other verbs:
qualcosa da mangiare something to eat
abbiamo we have
una limonata lemonade
un'aranciata orangeade
un caffè coffee
un tè tea
un'acqua minerale mineral water

ORDERING AND PAYING

11 A coffee

PAOLA	Buongiorno.
CAMERIERE	Buongiorno a lei.
PAOLA	Un caffè, per favore.
CAMERIERE	Un caffè . . . Pronti il caffè.
PAOLA	Grazie. Quant'è?
CAMERIERE	Novecento.

PAOLA   Grazie.
CAMERIERE   Grazie.

un cameriere a waiter; *una cameriera* a waitress
a lei to you; *buongiorno a lei* good day to you
pronti il caffè here is the coffee (*pronti* literally straight away, ready)
quant'è? how much is it?
novecento nine hundred

12   A cappuccino

PAOLA   Un cappuccino, per favore.
CAMIRIERE   Un cappuccino? . . . Ecco a lei il cappuccino.
PAOLA   Grazie. Quant'è?
CAMERIERE   Milledue.
PAOLA   Ecco.
CAMERIERE   Grazie.

un cappuccino espresso coffee with steamed, frothy milk
ecco a lei here you are; *ecco* here (it) is
milledue 1200; the complete form should be *milleduecento,* but prices are generally given in the shortened form

13   Tea, coffee and a cake

PAOLA   Buongiorno.
CAMERIERE   Buongiorno.
PAOLA   Un tè al limone e un caffè lungo, per favore.
CAMERIERE   Va bene. Un tè al limone e un caffè . . . Ecco
             a lei il tè al limone e il caffè lungo.
PAOLA   Grazie. E una brioche e una pasta anche.
CAMERIERE   Ecco a lei.
PAOLA   Grazie.

un tè al limone a lemon tea; tea with milk is *un tè al latte*
un caffè lungo (literally a long coffee), a weaker espresso

va bene fine, OK   *una pasta* a cake
una brioche a bun   *anche* too, also

Exercise 3 ☆
You order drinks and snacks at a café.

14 A coke and a beer

PAOLA	Buongiorno.
CAMERIERE	Buongiorno.
PAOLA	Una coca-cola e una birra, per favore.
CAMERIERE	Una coca e una birra. La coca, la birra media o piccola?
PAOLA	Piccola, per favore.
CAMERIERE	Piccola . . . una birra piccola, pronti.
PAOLA	Grazie, quant'è?
CAMERIERE	Tremila.
PAOLA	Ecco.
CAMERIERE	Grazie.

una birra a beer
la birra piccola o media? a small or medium beer?

15 A glass of wine

PAOLA	Buongiorno.
CAMERIERE	Buongiorno, signora.
PAOLA	Un bicchiere di vino bianco e un bicchiere di vino rosso.
CAMERIERE	Va bene.

un bicchiere a glass; *un bicchiere di vino* a glass of wine; *un bicchiere di latte* a glass of milk
bianco white; *rosso* red; *un bicchiere di vino bianco* a glass of white wine. Two more useful words when dealing with wine are *secco* dry, and *dolce* sweet; *un bicchiere di vino bianco secco* a glass of dry white wine.

Exercise 4 ☆ ☐☐
Listen to the cassette. Michele asks for advice before ordering
some glasses of wine. See if you can follow enough to fill in
the following wine table:

VINO	BIANCO	ROSSO	DOLCE	SECCO
Brachetto				
Soave				

Exercise 5 ☆
You order some drinks in a café. Listen to your tape for
instructions and answer.

EXPLANATIONS

SAYING HELLO AND GOODBYE

Buongiorno good day, and *buonasera* good evening, are used
both to greet and to say goodbye to people.
Ciao is used for informal greetings; with friends, or family,
but not with somebody you do not know well. Use the more
formal greetings in all shops and public places, and when
being introduced to somebody.
Arrivederci means goodbye, and is used at any time, with
anybody. You can use it followed by *buongiorno,* or *buonasera;
Arrivederci, buongiorno.*

NUMBERS

It is essential to learn them thoroughly; here they are again.

0 zero		
1 uno	100 cento	1000 mille
2 due	200 duecento	2000 duemila
3 tre	300 trecento	3000 tremila
4 quattro	400 quattrocento	4000 quattromila
5 cinque	500 cinquecento	5000 cinquemila
6 sei	600 seicento	6000 seimila
7 sette	700 settecento	7000 settemila
8 otto	800 ottocento	8000 ottomila
9 nove	900 novecento	9000 novemila
10 dieci		

You have also come across 11, *undici*.
1200 milleduecento; 2500 duemilacinquecento (sometimes in speech the *cento* is left out, so you will hear *milledue* and *duemilacinque* instead). More numbers appear on pages 44 and 94–5.

MASCULINE AND FEMININE

Words that represent people (e.g. man, woman, waiter), or objects (money, glass, etc.) are known as nouns.

In Italian, nouns are either masculine or feminine. Masculine nouns generally end in *-o (passaporto)* and feminine ones in *-a (birra)*; nouns ending in *-e (caffè, pensione)* are less predictable. This affects the articles ('the' and 'a') that accompany the words: in the dialogues you come across *un caffè* and *una pasta*, *un tè* and *una birra. Un* (masc.) and *una* and *un'* (fem.) are the three words for 'a'. Adjectives (words like 'good', 'old', 'green', 'fat', 'interesting', etc.) also change according to the gender of the noun: *un vino freddo* a cold wine; *una birra fredda* a cold beer.

WORTH KNOWING

CAFFÈ, BAR

Every Italian town possesses its own beloved old café or cafés, attractive, old-fashioned looking buildings which for centuries have been the center of the town's public life and gossip, and have witnessed its important cultural and political events. They may be more expensive than an ordinary bar, but are well worth visiting for a real taste of Italian life.

Bars are more recent institutions. Both bars and cafés sell alcoholic and non-alcoholic drinks, coffee, tea, and snacks, both sweet and savory.

Sometimes you will have to get the receipt (*lo scontrino*) at the cashier's before going to the bar and ordering. If you sit at a table *al tavolo*, you will get waiter service, *servizio al tavolo*, and may have to pay a lot more.

The *paninoteca* (sandwich bar) is a very recent development. The name comes from *panino* (roll) and it is frequented mostly by the very young, who gather outside rather than inside, to sip their cokes and eat the American-style hamburgers, or the many different kinds of *panini imbottiti* (filled rolls).

If you enjoy wine and would like to find out more about it, try an *enoteca*, a connoisseur wine cellar; here you can taste many different wines, especially local ones, bearing colorful and enticing names such as *fragolino* (strawberry-like), *dolcetto* (sweetish) and *vin santo* (holy wine).

DRINKS AND SNACKS

Coffee: *un caffè espresso* is a small cup of strong black coffee. *un caffè lungo* is slightly weaker. *un cappuccino* is an espresso with steamed, frothy milk.

un caffè corretto is a black coffee with a dash of either *grappa* or brandy.
un caffè macchiato is coffee with a dash of milk.

Tea: *un tè al latte* is tea with milk, but do ask for it *con latte freddo,* with cold milk, or you might be served boiled milk instead. Italians, however, prefer it *al limone,* with lemon, or, in the summer, they drink *tè freddo,* iced tea, served in a tall glass.

Chocolate: *una cioccolata calda,* hot chocolate, is generally served in the winter with whipped cream, *con panna.*

Sugar: *zucchero.*

Mineral water: *acqua minerale;* it can be either *naturale,* or *frizzante* (sparkling); you may also come across *gassata* for sparkling and *non gassata* for still.

Beer: Italian *birra* is generally lager-type, either brewed in Italy (*nazionale*) or a more expensive foreign brand (*estera*). It is always served cold.

Wine: *vino rosso* and *bianco.* Among the most famous white wines are Soave from Veneto, Tocai from Friuli and Verdicchio from Marche. Among the red ones are Barolo ('the King of wines') from Piedmont and Chianti from Tuscany.

Cakes: *una pasta* is the generic name for a small cake. In the morning it is customary to have *una brioche* with your *cappuccino;* this can contain *marmellata,* jam, or *crema,* custard cream, or it can be just plain, *normale.*

Snacks: *un salato,* or *salatino* (plural *salatini*) is an interesting change when you want a light bite: light pastry with cheese, spinach, anchovies or olives; a toasted sandwich is *un toast.*

Soft drinks: *aranciata* orangeade; *limonata* lemonade; *un frullato* a milkshake; *un succo di frutta* a fruit juice; *una spremuta* freshly squeezed fruit juice: *di limone* lemon; *di arancia* orange; *di pompelmo* grapefruit.

CAN YOU GET BY?

The exercises in this section will help you to check your progress. The answers to the exercises are on pages 105–112.

Exercise 1 ☐☐

WORD SEARCH. Can you find six expressions for greetings and thanks hidden in this puzzle? They are *buongiorno, buonasera, ciao, grazie, prego, per favore.* The puzzle works up and down, side to side, and backwards.

U	E	B	S	T	E	I	Z	A	R	G	O	M	P
L	N	U	A	R	P	C	C	D	F	H	A	N	Y
B	U	O	N	G	I	O	R	N	O	A	L	E	S
L	O	N	A	D	F	E	L	P	Q	S	U	I	T
O	L	A	R	T	D	D	S	O	A	F	I	L	R
R	I	S	T	O	P	E	R	F	A	V	O	R	E
Q	P	E	A	N	R	V	O	E	B	B	C	D	I
A	P	R	E	G	O	I	D	Z	Z	F	P	N	U
L	A	A	E	R	I	R	D	O	Z	P	S	V	V
V	L	Z	P	D	R	R	I	A	A	A	E	Q	P	Q
V	U	E	E	L	O	A	I	C	R	S	V	Z	H

Exercise 2 ☆ ▢▢
Bingo! Listen to the cassette, where Anna will call the numbers. Cross them out on the card below as you hear them. You should be left with one number at the end.

1		700		7
			900	
800		5		300
	8		400	
600		10		1000

Exercise 3 ☆ ▢▢
Read the exercise first, then switch on your cassette. Give your answers aloud.

1 You want to order a glass of sweet red wine. Which will you say . . . ?
a Un bicchiere di vino bianco dolce
b Un bicchiere di vino rosso dolce
c Un bicchiere di vino rosso secco

2 Now you want to order a medium-sized coke and a small beer. Which will you say . . . ?
a Una coca piccola e una birra media
b Una coca media e una birra piccola
c Una coca media e una birra media

3 You want to order a coffee laced with *grappa*. Which will you ask for . . . ?
a un caffè macchiato   **c** un caffè corretto
b un caffè lungo

4 Now you want something to eat. Which will you say . . . ?

a una pasta
b un'aranciata
c una spremuta

5 If you ask *Quant'è?*, which answer would you expect to hear . . . ?

a Uno, sette, cinque, otto, zero, due
b duemila
c grazie mille

2 SHOPPING

posso cambiare . . . ?	can I change . . . ?
un etto	100 grams
questo	this, this one
un pezzo di . . .	a piece of
basta (così)	that's enough
Ha . . . ?	Do you have . . . ?
quanto costa?	how much does it cost?
quanto costano?	how much do they cost?
troppo caro	too expensive
posso vederlo?	can I see it?

DIALOGUES

AT THE BANK

1 Changing a Eurocheque

FRANCESCA	Buongiorno.
IMPIEGATA	Buongiorno.
FRANCESCA	Posso cambiare un Eurocheque?
IMPIEGATA	Sì, certo. Al massimo di trecentomila lire.
FRANCESCA	Benissimo.
IMPIEGATA	Il suo documento?
FRANCESCA	Ecco.

un'impiegata a female employee; *un impiegato* is a male employee

posso can I?, may I?; *cambiare* to change; *posso cambiare . . . ?* can I change . . . ?

certo certainly

al massimo di trecentomila lire to a maximum of 300,000 lira

il suo your, yours

documento (literally document) identification, usually a passport

lira, plural *lire,* is the Italian currency – see the *Worth Knowing* section in this unit

2 Changing a traveler's check

STEPHANIE	Posso cambiare questo traveler's check, per favore?
IMPIEGATA	Sì, certo. È di cento sterline?
STEPHANIE	Sì.
IMPIEGATA	Bene. Il suo passaporto?
STEPHANIE	Ecco.
IMPIEGATA	Può firmare il suo traveler's check?
STEPHANIE	Ecco.
IMPIEGATA	Bene. Si accomodi in cassa. Arrivederci.
STEPHANIE	Arrivederci. Grazie, signora.

è is

di cento sterline for a hundred pounds; *una sterlina* (pl. *sterline*) one pound sterling; *un dollaro* (pl. *dollari*) one dollar

bene good (literally well)

un passaporto passport

può? can you? will you please?

firmare to sign; *può firmare?* can you sign?

si accomodi in this situation is a polite way to direct you to *la cassa,* the cashier's counter, but it is also used to show somebody in, and to get him or her to sit down; please sit down, make yourself comfortable.

Exercise 1 ☆

See how well you can get by at the bank. You want to change a Eurocheque and 100 dollars.

BUYING FOOD

3 Peaches

PAOLA	Buongiorno.
FRUTTIVENDOLO	Buongiorno.
PAOLA	Quattro pesche, per favore.
FRUTTIVENDOLO	Va bene. Tremila.
PAOLA	Grazie, ecco a lei.

il fruttivendolo the fruitseller
pesche peaches (sing. *una pesca*)

4 Rolls

PAOLA	Buongiorno.
NEGOZIANTE	Buongiorno.
PAOLA	Quattro panini, per favore.
NEGOZIANTE	Sì, subito . . . vuole normali?
PAOLA	Sì, questi, per favore.
NEGOZIANTE	Basta così?
PAOLA	Basta così, grazie.
NEGOZIANTE	Sei e cinquanta.

un, una negoziante shopkeeper
un panino a roll
normale ordinary
vuole? would you like?
questi these
basta così it is enough, that's all

5 200 grams of ham

SALUMIERE	Buongiorno, signora.

MARGHERITA	Buongiorno.
SALUMIERE	Mi dica.
MARGHERITA	Vorrei due etti di prosciutto.
SALUMIERE	Cotto o crudo?
MARGHERITA	Cotto. Questo.
SALUMIERE	Va bene.
MARGHERITA	Bene. Quant'è?
SALUMIERE	Cinquemila e trecento lire.

il salumiere works in *una salumeria,* selling cooked meats and salami, and often groceries as well
mi dica may I help you?; you will also hear *desidera?* and *prego?*
vorrei I'd like; you can use this phrase with verbs, too: *vorrei bere,* I'd like to drink. Another phrase for ordering is: *mi dà . . . ?* will you give me . . . ?
un etto 100 grams
il prosciutto ham
cotto cooked; *crudo* raw (i.e., cured, like Parma ham)

6 Cheese

MARGHERITA	Ha del formaggio?
SALUMIERE	No, mi dispiace.
MARGHERITA	Va bene, grazie.

7

GIULIA	Buongiorno.
SALUMIERE	Buongiorno.
GIULIA	Vorrei un pezzo di parmigiano, per favore.
SALUMIERE	Quanto?
GIULIA	Un etto.
SALUMIERE	Basta così?
GIULIA	Sì, grazie.
SALUMIERE	Dopo?
GIULIA	Basta, grazie.
SALUMIERE	Grazie a lei, molto gentile . . .

Ha . . . ? do you have?
del formaggio any/some cheese?
no, mi dispiace I am afraid not
un pezzo di parmigiano a piece of parmesan (this cheese is generally grated at home). If you want to say a little of, the expression is *un po' di.*
quanto? how much? *quanti?* how many?
dopo (literally) afterwards. Here are two other questions you will regularly be asked in shops; *altro?* anything else? *poi?* then?, next?
basta, grazie that's all, thanks
molto gentile very kind of you

Exercise 2 ☆
You are buying some ham, some cheese and some butter (*il burro*).

8   Ice cream

PAOLA	Buongiorno.
GELATAIO	Buongiorno, signorina.
PAOLA	Un gelato, per piacere.
GELATAIO	Un gelato, sì. Che gusto desidera?
PAOLA	(*pointing*) Eh, questo qui.
GELATAIO	Questo qui, eh, al limone?
PAOLA	Sì, grazie.
GELATAIO	Al limone. Pronti il gelato.
PAOLA	Quant'è?
GELATAIO	Mille.
PAOLA	Ecco.
GELATAIO	Grazie, arrivederci.
PAOLA	Buongiorno, grazie.

the *gelataio* works in *una gelateria* and sells *gelati* ice creams
signorina miss – now generally used with very young women
un gelato an ice cream

per piacere please (an alternative to *per favore*)
che gusto? what flavor?
desidera would you like
questo qui this one here

Exercise 3 ☆
Listen to another *gelataio* listing the flavors he sells. See if you can catch whether he sells peach-flavored ice cream and chocolate ice cream. (Transcript on page 107.)

AT THE PHARMACIST'S/CHEMIST'S

9

PAOLA	Buongiorno.
FARMACISTA	Buongiorno, signora.
PAOLA	Ha qualcosa per la diarrea?
FARMACISTA	Sì, queste gocce. Quindici tre volte al giorno.
PAOLA	Benissimo. Quant'è?
FARMACISTA	Eh . . . sono seimilanovecentocinquanta lire.
PAOLA	Ecco a lei.
FARMACISTA	Grazie.

una farmacista pharmacist works in a *farmacia* pharmacy
qualcosa per something for; *ha qualcosa per la diarrea?*
do you have anything for diarrhea?
gocce (sing., *goccia*) drops
quindici fifteen
volte times
al giorno per day; *tre volte al giorno* three times a day
benissimo very good (literally, very well)
sono seimilanovecentocinquanta lire it is 6,950 lire

AT THE TOBACCONIST'S

10 Buying *gettoni*

PAOLA	Buongiorno.
NEGOZIANTE	Buongiorno.
PAOLA	Ha dei gettoni, per favore?
NEGOZIANTE	Sì, certo, quanti?
PAOLA	Uno.
NEGOZIANTE	Eh, ecco, tenga.
PAOLA	Quant'è?
NEGOZIANTE	Eh, duecento.
PAOLA	Ecco a lei.
NEGOZIANTE	Grazie.
PAOLA	Grazie, buongiorno.
NEGOZIANTE	Buongiorno.

un gettone (pl. *gettoni*) a telephone token; *dei gettoni* some/any
telephone tokens
ecco tenga here it is (literally here, take it)

11 Buying a phone card

PAOLA	Buongiorno.
NEGOZIANTE	Buongiorno.
PAOLA	Ha delle carte telefoniche?
NEGOZIANTE	Sì. Da cinquemila, o da diecimila lire?
PAOLA	Una da cinquemila, per favore.
NEGOZIANTE	Ecco.
PAOLA	Grazie, buongiorno.
NEGOZIANTE	Buongiorno, grazie.

carta telefonica (pl. *carte telefoniche*) a phone card; *delle carte
telefoniche* some, any phone cards
da expresses value; *da cinquemila* a five thousand lire (phone
card)

12 Buying stamps

TABACCAIO	Buongiorno. Prego?
GIULIA	Buongiorno. Quanto costano i francobolli per lettera per l'Inghilterra?
TABACCAIO	Settecento lire per lettera.
GIULIA	E cartolina?
TABACCAIO	Seicento.
GIULIA	Venti francobolli per lettera per l'Inghilterra.
TABACCAIO	Allora, dieci e . . . venti. Quattordicimila.
GIULIA	Quattordici . . . ho ventimila.
TABACCAIO	Ecco, seimila di resto.
GIULIA E TABACCAIO	Grazie.

il tabaccaio the tabacconist; he works in *una tabaccheria*.
quanto costano . . . ? how much do (the stamps) cost?
un francobollo (pl. *francobolli*) a stamp; they are sold per *lettera*,
for letters, and *per cartolina,* for postcards
venti twenty
quattordici fourteen
Ho I have
(seimila) di resto (six thousand) change

Exercise 4 ☆
You buy telephone tokens, a phone card and stamps.

AT THE SHOPS
. . . .

13 Buying a present

PAOLA	Buongiorno.
NEGOZIANTE	Buongiorno, signorina.
PAOLA	Quanto costa questo portafoglio?
NEGOZIANTE	Questo portafoglio costa ottantacinque-mila lire.
PAOLA	Uhm . . . troppo caro. Ha qualcosa di . . . meno caro?

NEGOZIANTE	Sì, ho questo sempre in pelle e costa trentacinquemila lire. Oppure qualcosina che costa venticinque.
PAOLA	Posso vederlo?
NEGOZIANTE	Certo.
PAOLA	Va bene questo.
NEGOZIANTE	Bene. Le faccio un pacchettino?
PAOLA	No, grazie . . . Ecco venticinque.
NEGOZIANTE	Benissimo. Grazie.
PAOLA	Buongiorno, grazie.
NEGOZIANTE	Arrivederci, buongiorno.

quanto costa questo portafoglio? how much does this wallet cost? You can also use *quanto costa?* on its own to mean how much does it cost?

ottantacinquemila 85,000

troppo too, too much

caro dear, expensive

qualcosa something; *qualcosa di meno caro* something less expensive; another useful expression is *qualcosa di più grande,* something bigger

sempre still

in pelle in leather

trentacinquemila 35,000

oppure or (else)

qualcosina (the diminutive form of *qualcosa*) a little something

venticinque twenty-five

posso vederlo? may I see it? *vederlo* is a compound word formed of *vedere* to see, and *lo* it

le for you

Le faccio un pacchettino? Shall I gift-wrap it? *faccio* comes from *fare* to do or to make

un pacchettino is a diminutive for *pacchetto* (package)

· EXPLANATIONS ·

IL AND *LA*

il, l' and *lo* (masc.) and *la* and *l'* (fem.) are the Italian
equivalents of 'the'. *il* is used with most masculine words: *il
panino* the bread roll, *il telefono* the telephone. For masculine
nouns beginning with *sc. . ., st. . ., sp. . ., ps. . .* and *z* use *lo: lo
scontrino* the receipt, *lo zucchero* sugar.

la is used with most feminine words: *la pesca* the peach, *la carta*
the card.

l' is used for both masculine and feminine nouns beginning
with a vowel: *l'aranciata* or orangeade; *l'etto* 100 grams.

The plural of *il* is *i: i francobolli* the stamps; *i documenti* the
documents. The plural of *lo* is *gli: gli scontrini* the receipts.

The plural or *la* is *le: le lettere* the letters; *le cartoline* the
postcards.

DEL AND *DELLA*

del and *della* mean some, any: *Ha del formaggio?* Do you have
any cheese? *della limonata?* any lemonade? *Ha della birra?* Do
you have any beer?

The plural of *del* is *dei: Ha dei francobolli?* Do you have any
stamps? *Ha dei gettoni?* Do you have any tokens?

The plural of *della* is *delle: delle lettere* some letters; *Ha delle carte
telefoniche?* Do you have any phone cards?

PLURALS

You have come across the plurals of some nouns already: *lire,
pesche, panini*. In general, the masculine plural ends in *-i: il
panino, i panini*. The feminine plural usually ends in *-e: la
cartolina, le cartoline*.

Some words, particularly foreign words used in Italian, do
not change in the plural; *caffè* is one of them, and so is *bar: i
caffè, i bar*.

QUESTO, QUESTA

questo, questa is the word for 'this' and, like other adjectives, it changes according to whether the word it refers to is masculine or feminine, singular or plural: *questo portafoglio* (masc.) this wallet; *questa pasta* (fem.) this cake; *questi panini* (masc. pl.) these bread rolls; *queste pesche* (fem. pl.) these peaches.

QUANTO COSTA? QUANTO COSTANO?

costare means to cost. *costa* is the singular form: *questo portafoglio costa ottantacinquemila lire* this wallet costs 85,000 lire; *costano* is the plural form: *queste pesche costano tremila al chilo* these peaches cost 3,000 lire per kilo.
quant'è? and *quanto costa?* are more or less interchangeable, like 'How much is it?' and 'How much does it cost?' in English.

DA

da expresses value: *una carta telefonica da cinquemila* a five thousand lire phone card; it is used with notes *banconote,* and coins *monete: una banconota da diecimila lire,* a ten thousand lire note; *una moneta da cinquecento lire* a five hundred lire coin.

WORTH KNOWING

BANKS

Banks in Italy are open from Monday to Friday, generally between 8:30 in the morning until 1:30 in the afternoon. To change currency look for the sign *Cambio.* If you wish to cash a traveler's check you will need to show your passport. The clerk will probably take a photocopy of the first two pages of your passport; this is common practice, and should not alarm you! There may also be a small charge (*il bollo*). You may also be asked where you are staying: *Dove abita?* You only need to reply with the name of your hotel.

Most Italian banks are equipped with express service counters working 24 hours a day, which accept most Visa cards. Other places where you can change money are the *Aziende di Promozione Turistica* (APT), to be found in all main railway stations, and at tourist information centers (*Informazioni Turistiche*); as well as at the *Uffici Cambio* (exchange offices). These have different opening times, so beware!

MONEY

The Italian currency is the *lira* (written £, like the pound sterling), plural *lire*. Banknotes (*banconote*) come in denominations of 1,000, 2,000, 5,000, 10,000, 20,000, 50,000, and 100,000 lire. The main coins are 50, 100, 200, 500, and 1,000 *lire*.

POSTAL SERVICES

The main post office in Italy is called *Poste e Telecomunicazioni*. The initials PT appear on the sign marking an individual post office, *ufficio postale*. *L'ufficio postale* is generally open between 8:15 A.M. and 1:30 P.M. from Mondays to Fridays; 8:15 A.M. and 12:20 P.M. on Saturdays. Mail boxes are generally red, and bear two different slots; *per la città,* for local mail, and *per tutte le altre destinazioni,* for all other destinations. There are different postal rates in Italy: *per lettera,* for letters, and *per cartolina,* for postcards. You can get stamps also from tobacco shops, easily recognizable by their distinctive sign: a large white T. Ask for *francobolli per Stati Uniti* when you are writing to someone in the USA. Because Italians tend to subsume the whole of the United Kingdom under *Inghilterra* (England) people generally ask for *francobolli per l'Inghilterra*, regardless of where in the UK they are sending letters.

SHOPS

la farmacia is the pharmacy. Pharmacies are open Monday through Friday. If you need a pharmacist during the weekend or at night, you will find the emergency number (headed *farmacie di turno*) on the door of most pharmacies. Here is a list of the most common ailments, and how to ask for something to cure them; *ha qualcosa per . . . ?*

il mal di testa headache
il mal di stomaco stomachache
il mal di denti toothache
il raffreddore a cold

For some ailments, instead of tablets (*compresse*) you will be given *gocce,* drops, to be taken at regular intervals.

alimentari local grocer's shop

panetteria baker's, sells bread, flour, cakes, and cookies

pasticceria pastry shop

mercato market

supermercato supermarket

frutta e verdura is the greengrocer's. Here is a list of produce you may want to buy:

mele apples	*fragole* strawberries
banane bananas	*pomodori* tomatoes
arance oranges	*peperoni* peppers
pere pears	*carote* carrots
pompelmi grapefruit	*patate* potatoes

You will probably want to buy these by the kilo or half-kilo: *un chilo, mezzo chilo.*

macelleria butcher's shop

cantina wine shop

profumeria the perfumery, also sells cosmetics

valigeria leather-goods shop; a handbag is *una borsetta* and a belt is *una cintura*.

TELEPHONES

In Italy you can telephone from a public phone (*telefono pubblico*), from a bar, or from a hotel. If you are calling from your hotel room, you may have to ask to be given the line: *mi dà la linea?* can you give me the line?

Public phones take *gettoni* tokens, and/or coins: 100, 200, and 500 lire. Many also take *una carta telefonica* a phone card. You can get these, too, from a tobacconist.

The code for international calls is 00, followed by the code of the country (44 for Britain, 1 for the United States), then the area or town code (without the 0), and then the telephone number of the person you wish to call. So, to call the US number 516-434-3311 from Italy, you would dial 00-1-516-434-3311.

Italian numbers, after the code (*il prefisso*) have between five and seven digits; generally each digit is said individually, but sometimes people will couple them: *cinquanta* (50), *venti* (20) *undici* (11); 0 is *zero.*

Phone calls can be local, national (*teleselezione nazionale*), or international (*teleselezione internazionale*); 113 is the emergency number for police, ambulance, fire service, etc.

CAN YOU GET BY?

Exercise 1 ☆
See whether you can memorize Anna's shopping list!

Exercise 2 ☆
Some practice at understanding prices. (Transcript on page 107.)

Exercise 3 ☆ ☐ ☐
Read the exercise, and then work through it with the tape.

1   You are buying a wallet. Which will you say?
a   Vuole un portafoglio?
b   Vorrei un portafoglio.
c   Abbiamo un portafoglio.

2   You want to ask how much it costs. Will you say . . . ?
a   Quanto costano?
b   Quanto costa?
c   Questo qui?

3   You want to ask if they have something less expensive. Which will you say . . . ?
a   Ha qualcosa di meno grande?
b   Ho ventimila.
c   Ha qualcosa di meno caro?

4   You would like to see the cheaper wallet. Which will you say . . . ?
a   Posso cambiare?
b   Può firmare?
c   Posso vederlo?

5   How will you say 'This one's fine'?
a   Sì, certo. Quanti?
b   Va bene questo.
c   Cotto. Questo.

3 TRAVELING AROUND

KEY WORDS AND PHRASES

scusi?	excuse me?
dov'è?	where is?
ha una pianta della città?	do you have a map of the town?
per andare a . . . ?	the way to . . . ?
può ripetere?	can you repeat, please?
a destra	to the right
a sinistra	to the left
dritto	straight ahead
non ho capito	I have not understood
quale autobus?	which bus?
dove posso trovare i biglietti?	where can I get the tickets?
due biglietti per . . .	two tickets for . . .
un'andata	a one-way (ticket)
un'andata e ritorno	a round-trip ticket
prima classe	first class
seconda classe	second class
da che binario parte?	from which platform does it leave?
a che ora?	at what time?

DIALOGUES

ASKING THE WAY

1

GIULIA	Mi scusi, dov'è la toilette?
ALBERGATRICE	Al secondo piano.
GIULIA	Grazie.
ALBERGATRICE	Prego.

albergatrice hotelier (fem.)
mi scusi . . . ? excuse me . . . ? You can also simply say *scusi . . . ?*
dov'è . . . ? where is . . . ?
la toilette the toilet
al secondo piano on the second floor; on the first floor is *al primo piano*

2

FRANCESCA	Buongiorno.
IMPIEGATA	Buongiorno, signora.
FRANCESCA	Ha una pianta della città, per favore?
IMPIEGATA	Sì, eccola. Noi siamo qui in stazione; questo è il centro storico di Padova.
FRANCESCA	Dov'è il Duomo?
IMPIEGATA	È qui.
FRANCESCA	Grazie mille.
IMPIEGATA	Prego.

Ha una pianta della città? Do you have a street map of the city?
eccola here it is (*la* refers to *la pianta*)
noi siamo qui we are here; she is pointing at the map
in stazione at the station
il centro storico di Padova the historical center of Padua
il Duomo the cathedral

Exercise 1 ☆ □ □

Here are the names for some major cities. The presenter on the cassette will prompt you to ask for a map for some of them. For example: 'Do you have a street map of Padua?' is *Ha una pianta di Padova?*

Torino	Turin	*Venezia*	Venice
Milano	Milan	*Firenze*	Florence
Genova	Genoa	*Roma*	Rome
Padova	Padua	*Napoli*	Naples

See page 4 for a map of Italy.

3

FRANCESCA	Scusi, dov'è la fiera?
IMPIEGATA	Allora, fuori della stazione, a sinistra, sempre dritto; dopo il semaforo sempre dritto e subito a sinistra.
FRANCESCA	Grazie mille.
IMPIEGATA	Prego.

la fiera the trade fair
fuori della stazione outside the station
a sinistra on the left
sempre dritto straight ahead
dopo il semaforo after the traffic lights
subito a sinistra immediately left

4

STEPHANIE	Scusi, per andare a Santa Giustina, per favore?
GIULIA	Vada dritto, giri a sinistra, vada sempre dritto; dopo il semaforo, continui sempre dritto e sulla destra trova Santa Giustina.

per andare a Santa Giustina? to go to (the church of) Santa Giustina?

vada dritto go straight	*sulla destra* on the right
giri a sinistra turn left	*trova* you find
continui continue on	

5

Listen to Stephanie on the cassette asking the way to Vicenza.
See if you catch whether the sign indicating the direction for
Vicenza will be on the left or on the right.

STEPHANIE	Scusi, per andare a Vicenza, per favore?
GIULIA	Vada sempre dritto, al primo semaforo giri a a destra e continui sempre dritto. A un certo punto troverà un cartello sulla sinistra che indicherà la direzione per Vicenza.
STEPHANIE	Può ripetere, per favore. Non ho capito.
GIULIA	Vada sempre dritto, al primo semaforo giri a destra, continui sempre dritto e troverà un cartello sulla sinistra che le indica la direzione per Vicenza.
STEPHANIE	Grazie mille.
GIULIA	Prego.

al primo semaforo at the first lights
a un certo punto at one point
troverà you will find
un cartello a road sign
che indicherà which will indicate
la direzione the direction

per Vicenza to Vicenza
può ripetere? can you repeat?
non ho capito I have not
understood
che le indica that shows you

CATCHING A BUS

6

STEPHANIE	Quale autobus va alla stazione?
ISABELLA	Deve prendere l'autobus numero quattro.

quale autobus . . . ? which bus . . . ? *Quale autobus va alla
stazione?* Which bus goes to the station?
Deve prendere l'autobus numero quattro. You must take the
number 4 bus.

7

FRANCESCA	Scusi, l'autobus per il centro, per favore?
IMPIEGATA	Sì, allora, può prendere l'autobus numero tre, otto, o il diciotto.
FRANCESCA	Eh, grazie. Ehm, dove posso trovare i biglietti?
IMPIEGATA	I biglietti, fuori della stazione, subito a destra.
FRANCESCA	Grazie mille.
IMPIEGATA	Prego. Buongiorno.

l'autobus per il centro the bus for downtown
può prendere you can take
diciotto eighteen
dove posso trovare i biglietti? where can I get (literally find) the tickets? a ticket is *un biglietto*.

8

FRANCESCA   Due biglietti per l'autobus, per favore.

BUYING A TRAIN TICKET

9

— Un'andata per Bologna.
— Un'andata per Milano, per favore.

un'andata a single/one-way (ticket)

10

— Due biglietti per Verona, andata e ritorno . . . e in prima classe. Grazie.

andata e ritorno round-trip (ticket)
in prima classe (in) first class

11

— Un biglietto di andata per Firenze, con supplemento rapido.

con supplemento rapido with supplement; *un rapido* is an Intercity train; you may have to catch one for part of your journey, in which case you must also purchase *un supplemento rapido*.

— Roma, andata e ritorno, con supplemento rapido Firenze-Roma.
— . . . Cassino, andata e ritorno, con supplemento rapido tra Pisa e Roma.

tra between

Exercise 2 ☐☐
How would you say:

a a one-way to Rome, please.
b two round-trip tickets to Naples, first class.
c Venice, round-trip, with a supplement for the *rapido* train.

ASKING WHICH PLATFORM

12

FRANCESCA	Da che binario parte il treno per Feltre?
IMPIEGATO	Treno per Feltre, binario nove. Treno diretto Calalzo.
FRANCESCA	Grazie.
IMPIEGATO	Prego.

da che binario parte il treno? from which platform does the train leave?
il treno per Feltre the train to Feltre (a little Venetian town north of Venice)
diretto a direct line—as used here—you do not have to change trains. *Diretto,* however, is also a type of train (see *Worth Knowing* section for this unit).
Calalzo is the final destination of the train.

AT WHAT TIME?

Exercise 3 ☆

Learn how to tell the time in the *Explanations* section, and then write down the times read out by Anna and Alberto on the tape. You may also need to refer to the *More numbers* list in the same section. (Transcript on page 108.)

13

There is no Dialogue 13 in this unit.

14

FRANCESCA   A che ora parte il prossimo treno per Torino?
IMPIEGATO   Per Torino diretto non c'è. Alle undici e venti c'è un treno per Milano con coincidenza.
FRANCESCA   Ah, ho capito.

a che ora parte . . . ? at what time does . . . leave?
il prossimo treno per Torino the next train to Turin
c'è there is; *non c'è* there is not
alle undici e venti at 11:20
con coincidenza with a connection

15

FRANCESCA   A che ora arriva a Torino?
IMPIEGATO   L'arrivo è previsto a Milano alle tredici e quarantacinque, alle quattordici e dieci la coincidenza, a Torino alle quindici e cinquantasette.
FRANCESCA   Grazie mille.
IMPIEGATO   Prego.

a che ora arriva a . . . ? at what time does it arrive at . . . ?
l'arrivo è previsto per the arrival is scheduled for

Exercise 4 ☐ ☐ ☆

Listen to this exercise on the tape, and fill in the blanks in the timetable with the times of departure from Milano, the connection from Bologna and arrival in Firenze.

IL RITORNO   DA **MILANO–BOLOGNA** PER **FIRENZE**

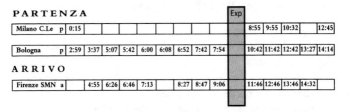

PARTENZA

											Exp						
Milano C.Le p	0:15											8:55	9:55	10:32		12:45	
Bologna p	2:59	3:37	5:07	5:42	6:00	6:08	6:52	7:42	7:54			10:42	11:42	12:42	13:27	14:14	

ARRIVO

											Exp						
Firenze SMN a		4:55	6:26	6:46	7:13		8:27	8:47	9:06			11:46	12:46	13:46	14:32		

BOOKING A SEAT

16

FRANCESCA	Vorrei un biglietto per Roma in prima classe con prenotazione.
IMPIEGATO	Va bene. Quando desidera partire?
FRANCESCA	Giovedì.
IMPIEGATO	Verso che ora?
FRANCESCA	Verso mezzogiorno.
IMPIEGATO	Abbiamo un rapido alle 12.59. Fumatori o non fumatori?
FRANCESCA	Non fumatori, grazie.
IMPIEGATO	Settantamila e seicento.

con prenotazione with a reservation
quando desidera partire? when would you like to leave?
giovedì on Thursday
verso che ora? at about what time?
mezzogiorno midday
fumatorio o non fumatori? smoking or nonsmoking?

17
Listen to the following announcement on the cassette; from which platform does the train for Bologna leave?

— È in partenza dal binario uno il treno diretto ventotto settantacinque delle ore dieci e cinquantasette per Terme Euganee, Monselice, Rovigo, Ferrara, Bologna/Parte dal binario uno il diretto ventotto settantacinque delle ore dieci e cinquantasette per Terme Euganee, Monselice, Rovigo, Ferrara, Bologna.

partenza departure; you will see the plural *partenze* on station departure boards
È in partenza il treno diretto ventotto settantacinque Stopping train number 2875 is on the point of departure
ore hours *delle ore dieci e cinquantasette* the 10:57 train
per for
Terme Euganee, Monselice, Rovigo and Ferrara are stations on the line between Padua and Bologna.

EXPLANATIONS

MORE NUMBERS

undici	11	sedici	16
dodici	12	diciassette	17
tredici	13	diciotto	18
quattordici	14	diciannove	19
quindici	15		
venti	20	venticinque	25
ventuno	21	ventisei	26
ventidue	22	ventisette	27
ventitré	23	ventotto	28
ventiquattro	24	ventinove	29
trenta	30	trentuno	31
quaranta	40	trentadue	32, etc.
cinquanta	50		

primo first
secondo second
Both take the same gender as the noun: *primo piano* first floor;
seconda classe second class; *secondo piano* second floor.
More numbers appear on pages 15 and 94–95.

ASKING THE WAY, *DOV'È?*

scusi and *mi scusi* both mean excuse me and are used for
apologizing, for addressing a stranger, and for asking people
to repeat what they have said ('Sorry?'). However, 'Excuse me,'
in the sense of 'May I come past please?,' is *Permesso*.

dov'è . . . ? where is . . . ?; *dov'è la Fiera?* where is the trade fair?;
dov'è la farmacia? where is the pharmacy?

c'è, there is, can be either a question: *c'è una farmacia?* is there a
pharmacy?, or a statement: *c'è un rapido alle 12:10.*

quale . . . ? which . . . ?; *quale autobus va alla stazione?* which
bus goes to the station?; *quale treno va a Bologna?* which train
goes to Bologna?

da quale . . . ? from which?; *da quale binario parte il treno?*
which platform does the train leave from?

per for; *il treno per Bologna* the train to Bologna
da from; *il treno da Bologna* the train from Bologna

dritto straight ahead; *sempre dritto* is continue straight ahead for
quite a distance (but is often misused as an equivalent of *dritto*);
sempre means always.
a sinistra left; *a destra* right; *sulla destra* is on the right, *sulla
sinistra* on the left.
la prima strada a destra the first road on the right, is often
abbreviated to *la prima a destra* the first on the right.

al semaforo at the lights
fino al semaforo as far as the lights

dopo il semaforo after the lights
al, fino and *dopo* can be used with other nouns, too: *al museo* at the museum; *fino alla stazione* as far as the station; *dopo la farmacia* after the pharmacy.

di of; *la pianta di Padova* the street map of Padova; when you want to say 'of the town' though, you must say *della città*.

IF YOU DON'T UNDERSTAND

scusi, può ripetere? excuse me, can you repeat that?
non ho capito I didn't understand
ho capito (lit., I understood) understand

TELLING THE TIME

Che ore sono? What time is it? All hours (*le ore*) are feminine and plural: *le due, le tre, le quattro,* etc except for *l'una* one o'clock. So, *sono le due* it is two o'clock; *sono le tre* it is three o'clock; *sono le quattro* it is four o'clock, but *è l'una* it is one o'clock.

È mezzogiorno (masc.) it is midday, noon
È mezzanotte (fem.) it is midnight
a mezzanotte at midnight
da mezzanotte from midnight
fino a mezzanotte until midnight

Officially, Italian time works on the basis of the 24 hour clock. Minutes are added to the hour: *le tre e venti* twenty past three; or subtracted: twenty to three is *le tre meno venti*
23.35 *le ventitré e trentacinque*
8.15 *le otto e quindici*
7.45 *le otto meno un quarto*
The expressions *un quarto* a quarter, and *mezzo/mezza* express the quarter hour and the half hour: *le dieci e un quarto* a quarter past ten; *le dieci e mezza* half past ten

mattina morning
pomeriggio afternoon
sera evening
notte night
oggi today
ieri yesterday

domani tomorrow
stamattina this morning
oggi pomeriggio this afternoon
questa sera this evening
dopo pranzo after lunch

WORTH KNOWING

GETTING AROUND

BY BUS
Un biglietto turistico is a tourist ticket that gives you unlimited access to all buses for 24 hours. It can be purchased from railway stations, tourist information centers, and tobacconists'. Prices vary from city to city.

Whether you need an ordinary ticket, or a tourist one, you must purchase it before getting onto the bus.

la fermata is the bus stop; when at the bus terminal, generally found outside railway stations, look for the word *corsia*.

BY TRAIN
There are three main categories of train:
locale (a stopping train)
diretto (a slightly faster train; stopping at most stations)
rapido (express train); the last can be an Intercity train (abbreviated IC), or a Eurocity train (abbreviated EC). For both you need to pay a supplement, *un supplemento;* for the EC, this cannot be below a certain sum. In some cases, you must also make a reservation in advance; some IC and EC trains also carry first class only. Check these details in the timetable, *l'orario.* Look for the words *partenze*

(departures) and *arrivi* (arrivals). Also, look for the abbreviation RTD on the departures board; it stands for *ritardo* delay. If your train is late, the delay time will appear on the board.

You get your ticket from the *biglietteria* the ticket office.

BY BICYCLE

Noleggio biciclette In many Italian towns and cities you can obtain a bicycle to get around downtown, free of charge. The service is in fact provided by the local council, *il Comune.* You only need your passport (or any other document proving your identity). Look for the sign *Noleggio biciclette* at the railway station, or ask at the information center. There may be several hiring points in the center of town too.

Two major offices will give you all the information you need about the city or town you are visiting: the *APT* offices (*Azienda di Promozione Turistica*), and the *IAT* offices (*Uffici di Informazione ed Assistenza Turistica*). The latter are to be found in all railway stations.

One last useful expression: *Buon viaggio!* Bon voyage!

CAN YOU GET BY?

Exercise 1 ☆
Listen to the recording of the switchboard operator giving you the opening times of an office. Between what times is it open in the afternoon? (Transcript on page 108.)

Exercise 2 ☐☐
Buying tickets for buses and trains

1   You want to buy a bus ticket for downtown. Which will you say?

a Due biglietti, per favore   **c** L'autobus per il centro,
b Un biglietto, per favore   per favore?

2 You want to ask which stop the bus leaves from. Which will you say?

a Da che binario parte?

b Dov'è il centro storico?

c Da che fermata parte?

3 You want to buy a second class, round-trip train ticket to Milan. Which will you say?

a Un'andata in seconda classe per Milano.

b Un biglietto di andate e ritorno, seconda classe, per Milano.

c Uno per Milano, per favore.

4 You want to leave today, at about two o'clock. Which will you say?

a Oggi, verso mezzogiorno.

b Domani, verso le due.

c Oggi, verso le due.

Exercise 3 ☆ ☐ ☐
Complete the following dialogue.

YOU	A one-way to Palermo in first class with a reservation.
IMPIEGATO	Quando desidera partire?
YOU	Tomorrow around midday.
IMPIEGATO	C'è un treno alle dodici e dieci.
YOU	Is there a supplement?
IMPIEGATO	Sì. Fumatori o non fumatori?
YOU	Non smoking, please.
IMPIEGATO	Va bene.
YOU	From which platform does the train leave?
IMPIEGATO	Dal binario numero tre.

Exercise 4 ☆ □□

Using the map, follow the three sets of directions given on the cassette, and see if you can work out where they are sending you each time.

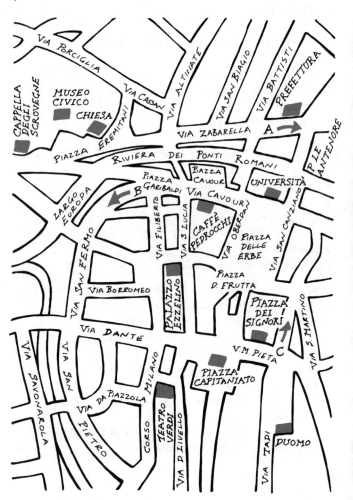

4 GETTING SOMEWHERE TO STAY

KEY WORDS AND PHRASES

ha una camera libera?	do you have a room free?
una camera singola	a single room
una camera doppia	a double room
una camera matrimoniale	a room with a double bed
una camera a due letti	a twin-bedded room
con bagno	with bathroom
senza bagno	without bathroom
con doccia	with shower
la colazione	breakfast
la chiave	the key
ho prenotato	I have booked
c'è anche un ristorante?	is there a restaurant, too?
un ostello della gioventù	youth hostel
avete posto?	do you have any room?
siamo . . .	we are . . .
un campeggio	campsite
c'è posto?	is there any room?
è all'ombra?	is it in the shade?

DIALOGUES

CHECKING INTO A HOTEL

A double room with bathroom

1

SERGIO	Buonasera.
ALBERGATRICE	Buonasera.
SERGIO	Ha una camera libera?
ALBERGATRICE	Eh . . . sì. Che tipo di camera?
SERGIO	Vorrei una matrimoniale con bagno.
ALBERGATRICE	Sì, va bene . . .

ha una camera libera? do you have a room free? The other word for room you will come across is *una stanza*.
che tipo di camera? What type of room?
una matrimoniale con bagno a double room with bathroom; *senza bagno* is without bathroom.

2

ALBERGATRICE	. . . per questa notte?
SERGIO	Sì. Quanto viene?
ALBERGATRICE	Il prezzo è centoeottomila lire, esclusa la colazione.
SERGIO	Benissimo.
ALBERGATRICE	Posso avere il suo documento?
SERGIO	Eccoli qua.
ALBERGATRICE	Eh . . . Grazie. Questa è la chiave della camera, la numero undici al primo piano.
SERGIO	Benissimo. Grazie.

per questa notte? for tonight?
quanto viene? (literally how much does it come out at?) is interchangeable with *quant'è?*
il prezzo the price
centoeottomila 108,000

esclusa la colazione breakfast excluded; breakfast included is
inclusa la colazione
posso avere il suo documento? may I have your document?
eccoli qua here they are (referring to the documents, e.g.
passports or identity cards)
la chiave the key
la numero undici number 11 (*la* refers to *la camera*)

A single room with shower
3

GIULIA	Buongiorno.
ALBERGATRICE	Buongiorno.
GIULIA	Ho prenotato una camera.
ALBERGATRICE	Sì. Il suo nome, per cortesia?
GIULIA	Puchetti.
ALBERGATRICE	Sì, la Signora Puchetti, è una camera singola con la doccia, per due notti.
GIULIA	Sì.
ALBERGATRICE	Giusto?
GIULIA	Sì.
ALBERGATRICE	Bene, allora, mi può lasciare il documento?
GIULIA	Eccolo qui.
ALBERGATRICE	Eh . . . Le dò la chiave, la camera è la numero trentatré al terzo piano. Si può accomodare.
GIULIA	Grazie.
ALBERGATRICE	Prego.

ho prenotato I have booked, reserved
il suo nome your name
per cortesia please, equivalent of *per favore*
una camera singola a single room
con la doccia with a shower
per due notti for two nights
giusto? is that right?
mi può lasciare il documento? can you leave me your identity

card (literally document)?
le dò la chiave I'll give you the key
al terzo piano on the third floor
si può accomodare is interchangeable with *si accomodi* please
make yourself at home.

Exercise 1 ☆ ☐ ☐
You are checking into a hotel; complete the dialogue on the
tape. Here are the details of your reservation:

NOME	SINGOLA	MATRIMON. CON BAGNO	MATRIMON. CON DOCCIA	NUMERO NOTTI
Martini			1	3

4

GIULIA	A che ora è la colazione?
ALBERGATRICE	Dalle sette e mezza alle dieci e mezza.
GIULIA	E . . . c'è anche un ristorante?
ALBERGATRICE	No, non abbiamo il ristorante, però posso consigliarle un ristorante qui vicino molto buono.

la colazione breakfast; lunch is *il pranzo*, and dinner *la cena*
dalle sette e mezza alle dieci e mezza from half past seven to half
past ten. From is *da*, and to is *a* but as times are always *le*, e.g.
le sette, le dieci, you say *dalle* and *alle*.
c'è anche un ristorante? is there also a restaurant?
però but
posso consigliarle I can recommend to you
qui vicino near here

Exercise 2 ☆ ☐ ☐
C'è anche . . . ? The presenter on the tape will prompt you to
ask this question using some of the following words and

expressions for hotel facilities. For example: *C'è anche una terrazza?* Is there also a balcony?

l'ascensore the elevator
la televisione the television
una vasca da bagno a bathtub
la piscina the swimming pool
l'aria condizionata air conditioning
la presa di corrente electrical socket/power point
il telefono the telephone
una terrazza a balcony
il servizio in camera room service
i servizi services, i.e. a toilet and a washbasin

MAKING A RESERVATION BY PHONE

5   (on the telephone)

ALBERGATRICE	Leon Bianco, buongiorno.
SERGIO	Buongiorno. Vorrei prenotare una camera.
ALBERGATRICE	Sì, per quando?
SERGIO	Per il 2 giugno.
ALBERGATRICE	Un attimo in linea, per cortesia . . . Il 2 giugno, eh, siamo al completo, mi dispiace.
SERGIO	Ho capito, grazie.
ALBERGATRICE	Prego, buongiorno.
SERGIO	Buongiorno.

Leon Bianco is the name of a famous hotel in Padua.
vorrei prenotare I would like to reserve
per quando? for when?
il 2 giugno June 2nd
un attimo in linea hold the line for one moment
siamo al completo we're fully booked

6

SERGIO	Buongiorno.

ALBERGATRICE	Buongiorno.
SERGIO	Io vorrei prenotare una camera doppia.
ALBERGATRICE	Sì. Per quando?
SERGIO	Per dopodomani.
ALBERGATRICE	Per dopodomani, dopodomani il 27 di maggio . . . eh . . . sì, posso prenotare una camera doppia. A due letti o matrioniale?
SERGIO	Eh, matrimoniale, grazie.
ALBERGATRICE	Sì, d'accordo. Soltanto per una notte?
SERGIO	Per due notti.
ALBERGATRICE	Per due notti. E quindi, domenica 27 e lunedì 28 maggio, partenza martedì 29.
SERGIO	Certo.

io I
per dopodomani for the day after tomorrow; tomorrow is *domani*
posso I can
a due letti with two beds
d'accordo OK, (literally agreed)
soltanto only
per una notte for one night
quindi then, therefore
domenica 27 Sunday 27th
lunedì 28 Monday 28th
maggio May
martedì 29 Tuesday 29th
For the remaining days of the week and months of the year, see the *Explanations* section for this unit.

Exercise 3 ☆
Listen to the recording on the cassette. How much would you pay for a twin room with a shower and breakfast for two? (Transcript on page 109.)

CHECKING INTO A YOUTH HOSTEL

7

STEPHANIE	Scusi, per andare all'ostello della gioventù, per favore?
GIULIA	Vada dritto, la prima strada a destra, la prima porta a sinistra, e là c'è l'ostello della gioventù.

l'ostello della gioventù the youth hostel
la prima porta the first door
là there, (literally in that place)

8

GIULIA	Buongiorno.
IMPIEGATO	Buongiorno.
GIULIA	Avete posto per questa notte?
IMPIEGATO	Sì, in quanti siete?
GIULIA	Siamo due ragazze e un ragazzo.
IMPIEGATO	Bene, allora mi servono i vostri passaporti.
GIULIA	Sì . . . tenga.
IMPIEGATO	Grazie.
GIULIA	C'è anche il ristorante?
IMPIEGATO	Sì. Il servizio ristorante incomincia alle otto di sera fino alle dieci.

avete posto per questa notte? do you have (any) space for tonight?
in quanti siete? how many of you are there?
siamo due ragazze e un ragazzo we are two girls and one boy;
ragazzo and *ragazza* are used for young people up to the age of 20.
mi servono i vostri passaporti I need your passports (literally your passports are useful to me)
il servizio ristorante the restaurant service
incomincia begins, starts
alle otto di sera at 8 o'clock in the evening
fino until

Exercise 4 ☆ □ □

Some reservations are being made at a youth hostel. Fill in the register page below specifying how many *ragazze* and how many *ragazzi* are booking in each time. Note that the page bears four different times, coinciding with each reservation. (Transcript on page 109.)

26 MAGGIO	RAGAZZI	RAGAZZE

CHECKING INTO A CAMPSITE

9

MICHELE	Buongiorno.
CUSTODE	Buongiorno.
MICHELE	C'è posto?
CUSTODE	Sì, certo.
MICHELE	Allora, siamo cinque persone: due adulti e tre bambini, con una roulotte ed una tenda.
CUSTODE	Ho il posto che fa al caso vostro.
MICHELE	È all'ombra?
CUSTODE	Sì, certo.
MICHELE	Molto bene. Eh . . . quanto costa? per quindici giorni?
CUSTODE	Quindici giorni ha detto . . . duecentocinquantamila lire.
MICHELE	Va bene. Allora lo prendo. Ecco i miei documenti.
CUSTODE	Va bene. Glieli dò domani.
MICHELE	Grazie.

c'è posto? is there (any) room?
siamo cinque persone there are five of us (literally we are five people)
adulti adults (sing. *un adulto*)
tre bambini three children (sing. *un bambino*)
una roulotte a caravan
una tenda a tent
Ho il posto che fa al caso vostro I have the space which suits your requirements
È all'ombra? Is it in the shade?
ha detto you said
lo prendo I'll take it
i miei documenti my documents
glieli dò domani I'll give them back to you tomorrow.

Exercise 5 ☆
You make a reservation at a campsite. Listen to your tape for instructions and answer.

Exercise 6 ☆ ▢
On the cassette, Anna tells you where she will be working next year. Fill in the time-planner in the book with the English place-names. (Transcript on page 109.)

DIARIO	
GENNAIO	LUGLIO
FEBBRAIO	AGOSTO
MARZO	SETTEMBRE
APRILE	OTTOBRE
MAGGIO	NOVEMBRE
GIUGNO	DICEMBRE

EXPLANATIONS

DATES

Dates are always masculine in Italian. The first of any month is *il primo . . . : il primo giugno* June 1; after that, dates are not second, third, fourth, but two, three, etc: *il due giugno, il tre giugno;* you will also hear *il due di giugno, il tre di giugno,* etc.

DAYS OF THE WEEK

I giorni della settimana The days of the week

lunedì	Monday	*venerdì*	Friday
martedì	Tuesday	*sabato*	Saturday
mercoledì	Wednesday	*domenica*	Sunday
giovedì	Thursday		

MONTHS OF THE YEAR

I mesi dell'anno The months of the year

gennaio	January	*luglio*	July
febbraio	February	*agosto*	August
marzo	March	*settembre*	September
aprile	April	*ottobre*	October
maggio	May	*novembre*	November
giugno	June	*dicembre*	December

SEASONS

Le stagioni The seasons

primavera	spring	*autunno*	autumn
estate	summer	*inverno*	winter

orario estivo summer timetable
orario invernale winter timetable

aperto open
chiuso closed
chiuso per ferie closed for holidays
chiuso per turno weekly closing (day)
chiuso per lutto closed for mourning

QUANTO?

quanto? how much? takes the gender and number of the words it accompanies: *per quanto?* for how long? *per quante notti?* for how many nights? *per quanti giorni?* for how many days?

PER

per indicates duration: *per due notti* for two nights; *per tre giorni* for three days; *per un'ora* for one hour; *per sei mesi* for six months; *per questa notte* for tonight; *per domani* for tomorrow; *per il ventotto di maggio* for May 28; *per quando?* for when?; *per* is also used with quantities: *per due persone* for two people

DA . . . A

da . . . a from . . . to: *da lunedì a venerdì* from Monday to Friday; *aperto dal lunedì al venerdì* open from Monday to Friday (every week).
dal . . . al are used with dates, which are masculine: *dal due al tre di settembre* from the second to the third of September; *dal ventuno di luglio al sei agosto* from the twenty-first of July to the sixth of August.

IN QUANTI SIETE?

in quanti siete? how many are you? (2nd person plural form)
siamo we are: *siamo tre ragazzi* we are three boys; *siamo in tre* there are three of us, (literally we are three)

un ragazzo (pl. *ragazzi*) a boy
una ragazza (pl. *ragazze*) a girl
un bambino child (masc.)
una bambina child (fem.)
bambini children
un adulto (pl. *adulti*) an adult
una persona (pl. *persone*) a person

HA . . . ?

ha? do you have? *ha una camera?* do you have a room?
avete? do you (plural) have?
ce'è . . . ? is there?; *ci sono . . . ?* are there?; *c'è posto?* is there
any room?; *ci sono bambini?* are there any children?
c'è is also used in statements: *c'è posto per oggi* there is room
(for) today

CON, SENZA

con with: *con doccia* with a shower
senza without: *senza bagno* without a bath

WORTH KNOWING

GETTING A HOTEL ROOM

If you haven't booked in advance, you can get advice from the
ATP and IAT offices already mentioned in the previous
chapter.

pensione completa full board
mezza pensione half board
colazione breakfast
colazione inclusa breakfast included
colazione esclusa breakfast excluded

pranzo is the main meal of the day, generally consumed at lunch time

cena is the evening meal and can either be a formal meal or just supper

Hotels are now generally classified according to the international star code, but you still find them classified in first, second and third category: *di prima, seconda e terza categoria.*

Pensioni offer more modest accommodation.

Ostelli della gioventù youth hostels have greatly developed in Italy over the past ten years. Every major town has one. They are well-run, cheap and pleasant.

Tourist attractions: museums and art galleries are generally closed on Mondays; for some monuments, however, as well as major exhibitions, you must book your visit in advance. APT offices will generally be able to help you with the bookings.

CAN YOU GET BY?

Exercise 1 ☐☐ ☆

"Thirty days hath September . . ." Fill in the blanks with the correct month and then list the months with 31 days *before* you listen to the solution on the cassette (the order of the months is slightly different from that in the English rhyme). (Transcript on page 110.)

Trenta giorni ha n . . . . . . , con a . . . . . . , g . . . . . . e s . . . . . . ; di ventotto ce n'è uno (f . . . . . .); tutti gli altri ne han trentuno.

Exercise 2 ☆ ☐☐ (answers on the tape only)

How would you say

a A single for the 25th of August?

b   A double with bathroom for the 2nd, the 3rd and the 4th of July?

c   A double room with shower for fifteen days?

d   Is there room for the 10th of September?

e   Is it in the shade?

f   Is there a restaurant?

g   Do you have room for the day after tomorrow?

h   We are three girls and two boys.

5 EATING OUT

KEY WORDS AND PHRASES

ci porta . . . ?	can you bring us?
il menù	the menu
l'antipasto	starters
il primo	the first course
il secondo	the second course
il contorno	vegetables or salad
il dolce	dessert
prendo	I'll have
mi porti	bring me
prendiamo	we'll have
per me	for me
per . . .	for . . .
cos'è . . . ?	what is . . . ?
le piace?	do you like?
mi piace	I like
preferisco . . .	I prefer . . .
niente dolce, grazie	no dessert, thank you
il conto	the bill

MENU A

Ristorante Al Pero – Padova

PIATTI DEL GIORNO	DISHES OF THE DAY
Zuppa di verdura	vegetable soup
Tagliatelle in brodo	tagliatelle in broth
Riso al pomodoro	rice with tomatoes
Spaghetti al ragù	what we call "spaghetti bolognese"
Spaghetti al tonno	spaghetti with tuna fish sauce

CONTORNI	SIDE DISHES
Insalata mista	mixed salad
Insalata verde	green salad

MENU B

Ristorante Da Taparo – Torreglia

ANTIPASTI

Salmone con crostino	Salmon with hot buttered toast
Prosciutto e melone	Ham and melon
Antipasto della casa	The "House" appetizer

PRIMI PIATTI

Risotto all'ortica	Nettle risotto
Risotto agli asparagi	Asparagus risotto
Risotto alla quaglia	Quail risotto
Bigoli alle salse	Home-made, thick spaghetti with a choice of sauces

Gnocchi alle salse	Small dumplings with a choice of different sauces
Zuppa di asparagi	Asparagus soup
Pappardelle agli asparagi	Asparagus pappardelle (a type of pasta)
Pasta e fagioli	Pasta and bean soup
Tagliatelle alle erbe	Herb tagliatelle

SECONDI PIATTI

Filetto alle erbe	Fillet of beef with herb sauce
Braciola di vitello	Veal chop
Braciola di maiale	Pork chop
Tagliata di manzo	Boiled beef served with sauces

DIALOGUES

ORDERING PIZZA

1

EMANUELA   Ci porta cinque pizze, per favore . . . ? allora
. . . una margherita, due ai funghi, una quattro
stagioni senza cipolla, e una quattro stagioni
con cipolla. Grazie.

ci porta will you bring us
una margherita is the basic pizza with tomato sauce and cheese
ai funghi with mushrooms
una quattro stagioni (literally a four seasons) pizza divided into
four sections, with four different toppings
senza cipolla without onions

ASKING FOR THE MENU IN A *TRATTORIA*

2

GIULIA   Buongiorno.

CAMERIERE   Buongiorno.

GIULIA   Ci porta il menù, per favore?

CAMERIERE   Certo . . . Ecco a lei.

GIULIA   Grazie . . . E da bere . . . una bottiglia di
acqua minerale.

CAMERIERE   Gassata o non gassata?

GIULIA   Non gassata.

CAMERIERE   Bene.

GIULIA   Grazie.

ci porta il menù? will you bring us the menu?
da bere to drink
una bottiglia di acqua minerale a bottle of mineral water
gassata sparkling, an alternative to *frizzante; non gassata* still

ORDERING LUNCH

3

GIULIA   Allora, un piatto di spaghetti al pomodoro,
un risotto di asparagi, un'insalata verde e dei
pomodori all'olio.

CAMERIERE   Va bene.

un piatto di spaghetti a dish of spaghetti
al pomodoro with tomato sauce
un'insalata verde lettuce, (literally green salad)
dei pomodori all'olio sliced tomatoes dressed in olive oil
There is a list of types of pasta in the *Explanations* section for
this unit.

ASKING FOR THE BILL

4

GIULIA   Il conto per favore.
CAMERIERE   Va bene.

il conto the bill

Exercise 1 ☆ ☐ (answers on the tape only)
You are ordering lunch in a *trattoria*. Consult Menu A on page 66 for your order.

ORDERING DINNER

5

CAMERIERE   I signori, che cosa prendono?
SIG. BORGHESAN Come antipasto, prendo un antipasto della
               casa. E come primo piatto, una zuppa di
               asparagi, e come secondo prendo un filetto
               alle erbe . . .

I signori, che cosa prendono? What will the gentleman have?
come antipasto as an appetizer/starter
prendo I will have
un antipasto della casa the restaurant's own special appetizer (*della casa*, literally of the house, of the restaurant)
come primo piatto for the first course; *il primo piatto*, the first course, is often abbreviated to *il primo*.
una zuppa di asparagi asparagus soup
come secondo for the second course; *il secondo piatto* is also abbreviated to *il secondo*.
un filetto alle erbe fillet steak in herb sauce

6

MICHELE   Per me invece, del prosciutto e melone, per
               antipasto; gli gnocchi di patate alle salse,
               come primo e . . . una braciola di vitello,
               come secondo . . .

per me for me
invece (literally instead) on the other hand
del prosciutto e melone ham (generally Parma) with melon
gli gnocchi di patate potato dumplings
alle salse with a choice of different sauces
una braciola di vitello a veal chop

7

CAMERIERE	Un po' di insalata di contorno?
SIG. BORGHESAN	Sì.
MICHELE	Sì. Per me dell'insalata verde, grazie.
CAMERIERE	Prende del vino bianco o del vino rosso?
MICHELE	Del vino bianco secco.
SIG. BORGHESAN	Bene . . . anch'io del vino bianco secco.
CAMERIERE	Abbiamo del vino della casa, ottimo . . .
SIG. BORGHESAN	Va molto bene il vostro vino della casa.
CAMERIERE	Dell'acqua minerale?
MICHELE	Per me dell'acqua minerale gassata.
SIG. BORGHESAN	Anche per me.
CAMERIERE	Grazie.

insalata di contorno side salad as your accompanying vegetable;
contorno is usually any vegetable served with a main course.
vino della casa house wine, also the restaurant's own home-
made, or home-bottled wine
ottimo excellent
anche per me for me, too

Exercise 2 ☆ ☐ ☐
Consult Menu B on pages 66–67. On the tape, one of the
waiters will say which of the first courses are available today.
Check them off on the menu. (Transcript on page 110.)

MAKING CONVERSATION

8

MICHELE   Buon appetito!
SIG. BORGHESAN   Buon appetito!

9

SIG. BORGHESAN   Le piace la braciola di vitello?
MICHELE   Molto buona, grazie. E il suo filetto?
SIG. BORGHESAN   Buonissimo.

le to you
le piace? do you like? (literally does it please to you?) *Le piace la braciola?* Do you like the chop? The reply is *sì, mi piace* yes, I like it.
molto buona very good
buonissimo excellent

ORDERING THE DESSERT

10

CAMERIERE   E come dolce, che cosa prendono? Abbiamo una torta alle mele, abbiamo della torta alle mandorle, della torta alla ricotta . . .
SIG. BORGHESAN   Prendo una torta alle mele.
MICHELE   Per me niente dolce, grazie. Preferisco un caffè.

come dolce for dessert
torta alle mele apple tart
torta alle mandorle almond cake
torta alla ricotta a cake made with ricotta cheese
niente dolce no dessert
preferisco I prefer

EXPLANATIONS

ORDERING A MEAL

Ci porta . . . ? Will you bring us . . . ? *ci* means to us
cosa prendono i signori? what will the (ladies and) gentlemen
take?, what will you have?
prendo I'll have
prendiamo we'll have

per me for me; *per la signora* for the lady; *per il signore* for the
gentleman

io I; *io prendo* I'll have; *io vorrei* I would like

come primo for starters
come secondo for second course
come contorno as a side dish

cos'è? what is it? You might want to use this expression to
inquire abou the name of a dish you cannot understand: *Cos'è
il baccalà alla vicentina?* what is *baccalà alla vicentina?* It is a fish
dish: cod boiled in oil and milk, a speciality from Vicenza.
Here are other questions you may want to ask:

è carne? is it meat?
è pesce? is it fish? (beware: *pesce* fish, and not *pesche* peaches!)
è salato? is it savory/salty?
è dolce? is it sweet?
è piccante? is it spicy?
è con l'aglio? does it have garlic?

sono vegetariano (masc.)/*sono vegetariana* (fem.) I am vegetarian

non posso mangiare I cannot eat; *non posso mangiare carne* I cannot
eat meat; *non posso mangiare cipolla* I cannot eat onion

le piace? do you like it? (literally is it agreeable to you?) *le piace
il risotto?* do you like risotto? *le piace la pizza?* do you like pizza?

mi piace I like it; *mi piace il risotto* I like risotto
non mi piace I don't like it; *non mi piace la cipolla* I don't like
onion

preferisco I prefer; *preferisco un caffè* I prefer a coffee

TYPES OF PASTA

Pasta comes in many different shapes and sizes: short, like
penne quills or *tortiglioni;* long, like *spaghetti, tagliatelle,
maccheroni, bigoli* (home-made spaghetti), *fettuccine* (thinner
tagliatelle). Pasta for oven-baking includes *lasagne* and
cannelloni; meat or cheese-filled pasta includes *tortellini* (with
meat), *tortelloni* (bigger, filled with spinach and ricotta cheese)
and *ravioli* (meat or ham).
Remember! Pasta names are always plural! *le tagliatelle, le
lasagne!* If you say *la lasagna,* it means one sheet of pasta only!

Pasta dishes are served with sauces; *al pomodoro* with tomato
sauce: *al ragù* what we call bolognese sauce; *al pesto* a
herbal sauce made with fresh basil, pine nuts, and garlic,
a speciality from Genoa. *Al, alla, ai* refer to the main
ingredients of the sauce: *pizza ai funghi* pizza with
mushrooms. They can also refer to the method of cooking: *al
forno* oven-cooked; *ai ferri* or *alla griglia* grilled; and to the style
of preparation: *pasta e fagioli alla veneta* pasta with beans in the
style of the Veneto region; *saltimbocca alla romana* veal and ham
cooked in the Roman style; *fegato alla veneziana* liver fried in
onion and white wine, in the Venetian style, etc.

WORTH KNOWING

PLACES TO EAT

The most expensive kind of restaurant calls itself *un ristorante.*
If you are looking for something cheaper, look for *una*

trattoria, a small family restaurant. Sometimes, however, you can find both words together: *ristorante trattoria,* and the price can sometimes be the same as in *un ristorante. Trattorie* generally specialize in regional cooking, so they are worth trying! You can eat more cheaply in *una tavola calda,* a small self-service restaurant, or in *una rosticceria,* generally a high-quality take-out specializing in roast dishes, where it is often possible to eat on the premises. *La pizzeria* is sometimes not the most obviously cheap place to eat!

When eating in *ristoranti* or *trattorie,* avoid the *menù turistico,* the fixed-price meal, and be adventurous and try any *specialità regionale,* a dish typical of a particular region. Italian food is extremely varied, and even if you order a dish with an incomprehensible name, you are likely to eat something tasty!

An Italian meal consists generally of *il primo (piatto)* the first course, a soup, a pasta or rice dish; *il secondo (piatto)* the second course, meat or fish; *il contorno* a side dish of mixed vegetables or salad; *il dolce,* or *il dessert,* a dessert. You also have *l'antipasto* starters, which varies greatly according to the type of cuisine and restaurant: *antipasto di pesce* fish antipasto; in the menu reproduced in this unit, Sig. Borghesan asks for *un antipasto della casa* the 'house' *antipasto.* It is always advisable to try recipes, wine, etc. of the house, if on offer: *vino della casa* house wine; *dolce della casa* house dessert, etc.
coperto the cover charge
la mancia the tip

NON-PASTA DISHES

Rice dishes are typical of Northern Italy; risotto recipes are infinite! *Risotto alla quaglia* quail risotto; *risotto alla milanese* risotto with saffron in the Milanese style; *risotto agli asparagi* asparagus risotto; *risotto ai funghi* mushroom risotto, etc.

Misto often appears in the names of dishes; *insalata mista* mixed salad; *bollito misto* mixed boiled meats, served with different sauces.

Other types of meat dishes are:

braciola di maiale pork chop	*pollo* chicken
braciola di vitello veal chop	*faraona* guinea-fowl
cotoletta cutlet	*quaglia* quail
filetto fillet	*anitra* duck
bistecca steak	*galletto* spring chicken

Fish dishes include:

fritto misto mixed fried seafood	*tonno* tuna
trota trout	*seppie* cuttlefish
zuppa di pesce fish soup	*salmone* salmon

Il contorno consists generally of vegetables:
patate fritte French fries
patate arroste roast potatoes
fagiolini string beans
spinaci spinach
verdure cotte mixed boiled vegetables (spinach, fennel, artichoke, etc.)

Il dolce is the dessert and includes cakes, mousses, ice creams etc. The word also means 'cake', so you can come across *il dolce della casa,* as well as *la torta della casa.* The difference is that torta only means cake: *la torta alla ricotta* ricotta cheesecake.

Buon appetito! Bon appetit!

CAN YOU GET BY?

Exercise 1 ▢▢

Complete the following puzzle:

(Horizontal)

1 One who does not eat meat (masc.)

(Vertical)

2 Salmon is . . .

3 Beef is . . .

4 I like

5 Sweet

6 They come with the second course

Exercise 2 ▢▢

a one of these places is not meant for eating:

forno   trattoria   rosticceria   tavola calda

b one of these is not meant to be eaten:

funghi   pappardelle   verdure   cameriere

c which of these would not be a pasta dish?

lasagne   bigoli alle salse   tagliatelle al ragù   tagliata di manzo

d which one of these would you not ask the waiter?

è piccante?   è dolce o secco?   senza cipolla, per favore   Le piace la sua braciola di vitello?

e If you can't eat garlic, which of these dishes would be suitable for you?

torta alla ricotta   pizza quattro stagioni   maiale arrosto pasta al pesto

Exercise 3 ☆

Cos'è . . . ? You inquire about a dish you have not tried
before.

Exercise 4 ☐☐ ☆

You are having a business dinner. Consult Menu B on page
66–7, and fill in the parts for both host and client.

CAMERIERA	Buonasera.
HOST	Good evening. Will you bring us the menu, please?
CAMERIERA	Subito . . . eccolo.
	(She then returns to take your order.)
	Cosa prendono?
CLIENT	As a starter, I'll have ham and melon.
HOST	For me too, please.
CAMERIERA	E come primo?
CLIENT	I'll have quail risotto.
CAMERIERA	È ottimo. E per lei?
HOST	For me, asparagus soup.
CAMERIERA	E poi?
CLIENT	The fillet with herbs – is it spicy?
CAMERIERA	No.
CLIENT	Then I'll have it.
CAMERIERA	Va bene. E per lei?
HOST	For me, as a second course . . . a veal chop.
CAMERIERA	Bene. Di contorno?
CLIENT	A green salad.
CAMERIERA	Anche per lei?
HOST	No – for me a mixed salad, please.

6 MEETING PEOPLE & DOING BUSINESS

KEY WORDS AND PHRASES

sono . . .	I am . . .
vorrei parlare con . . .	I'd like to speak to
il direttore	the managing director
quando torna?	when does he/she get back?
può richiamarmi?	can he/she call me back?
pronto?	hello?
ho un appuntamento con . . .	I have an appointment with
le presento	may I introduce
piacere	how do you do?
fissare un appuntamento	to arrange an appointment
la mia collega	my colleague
mia moglie	my wife
mio marito	my husband
sono occupato	I am busy
sono in ritardo	I am late
come sta?	how are you?
bene	well
di dov'è?	where are you from?
inglese	English
prenotare una macchina	to reserve a car
carta di credito	credit card
il nome è . . .	the name is . . .

DIALOGUES

MAKING A PHONE CALL
....

1

SEGRETARIA   Zanetti Group, buongiorno.
SIG. GERMANO   Buongiorno. Vorrei parlare con il direttore.
SEGRETARIA   Il direttore non è in ufficio. Chi parla?
SIG. GERMANO   Sono Attilio Germano, della Lori . . .

Zanetti Group is the name of the firm/company
parlare speak; *vorrei parlare con* I'd like to speak to, (literally with)
il direttore the director
non è is not; *non è in ufficio* he's not in the office
chi parla? lit. who's speaking?
sono I am
della Lori of Lori's; Lori is the name of Germano's firm (*ditta*);
della refers to *la ditta Lori* the firm, Lori.

2

GERMANO   Quando torna?
SEGRETARIA   Può richiamare tra un'ora?
SIG. GERMANO   Va bene, grazie.
SEGRETARIA   Prego, buongiorno.
SIG. GERMANO   Buongiorno.

quando torna? when is he coming back?
richiamare to call back; *può richiamare?* can you call back?
tra un'ora in an hour's time

3

SEGRETARIA	Zanetti Group, buongiorno.
GERMANO	Buongiorno. Vorrei parlare con il direttore.
SEGRETARIA	Mi dispiace, signor Germano, il direttore è occupato.
GERMANO	Può richiamarmi?
SEGRETARIA	Sì. Mi lascia il suo numero?
GERMANO	Sì. Zero sette uno novantuno tredici ottantacinque.
SEGRETARIA	Eh . . . scusi . . . può ripetere?
GERMANO	Zero sette uno novantuno tredici ottantacinque.
SEGRETARIA	La ringrazio molto, buongiorno.
GERMANO	Buongiorno.

è occupato he's busy
può richiamarmi can he call me back?
mi lascia will you leave me
novantuno ninety one
la ringrazio molto (I) thank you very much

4

SEGRETARIA	Lori, buongiorno.
ZANETTI	Il signor Germano, per favore?
SEGRETARIA	Chi devo dire?
ZANETTI	Zanetti.
SEGRETARIA	Rimanga in linea, per favore. Glielo passo subito.

chi devo dire? who should I say?
rimanga in linea hold the line
glielo passo subito I'll put him through to you immediately

Exercise 1 ☆ ☐☐ (answer on the tape only.)
You telephone the Lori company – here is your telephone number: 044 68 48 16.

5

SEGRETARIA	Buongiorno.
GERMANO	Buongiorno. Sono Attilio Germano, della ditta Lori. Ho un appuntamento con il signor Zanetti.
SEGRETARIA	A che ora?
GERMANO	Alle cinque.
SEGRETARIA	Si accomodi pure.
GERMANO	Grazie.
SEGRETARIA	Gli dico subito che è arrivato.

ho un appuntamento con I have an appointment with
Si accomodi pure do sit down
gli dico I'll tell him
che è arrivato that you have arrived

6

ZANETTI	Il signore Germano?
GERMANO	Sì.
ZANETTI	Eh . . . Sono Zanetti, buongiorno.
GERMANO	Piacere.
ZANETTI	Le presento la mia collega, la signora Bianchi.
GERMANO	Piacere.

piacere how do you do (literally pleasure, my pleasure)
le presento may I introduce, (literally I introduce to you)
la mia collega my colleague (fem.); *il mio collega* (masc.)

7

SEGRETARIA	Zanetti Group, buongiorno.
GERMANO	Buongiorno. Sono Attilio Germano, vorrei fissare un appuntamento con la signora Bianchi.
SEGRETARIA	Attenda un attimo . . . che controllo. Domani pomeriggio va bene? . . . o . . . mercoledì?

GERMANO	Ehm . . . mercoledì sono occupato. Martedì?
SEGRETARIA	Martedì pomeriggio . . . va bene.
GERMANO	Bene, grazie.
SEGRETARIA	A che ora?
GERMANO	Verso le tre?
SEGRETARIA	Alle tre, va bene. D'accordo.
GERMANO	Grazie, buongiorno.
SEGRETARIA	Buongiorno.

fissare un appuntamento con . . . to arrange (literally to fix) an appointment with . . .
attenda un attimo . . . (please) wait a moment
che controllo . . . (literally that I check) while I check
d'accordo agreed

Exercise 2 ☆ ☐ ☐
Here is a page of your diary. Which day can you manage for your appointment with signora Rossi?

LUNEDÍ	GIOVEDÍ
Roma – treno 7:45	Appunt. Lori 11:30
MARTEDÍ	**VENERDÍ**
Roma	Pranzo 13:00
MERCOLEDÍ	**SABATO**
Ritorno treno 15:00 Appunt. Zanetti 17:00	—

Exercise 3 ☆ ☐ ☐
Record the following message on Zanetti's *segreteria telefonica* (answering machine) in Italian:
Hello, I am Vivian Stewart, the owner of Stewart Software. I'd like to arrange an appointment with the marketing director. Can he call me back? My number is 02 31 81 82 75. I am in the office tomorrow morning. Thank you, good day.

MEETING PEOPLE

8

CRISTINA	La signora Fisher?
SIG.RA FISHER	Sì . . .
CRISTINA	Sono Cristina Degani, piacere.
SIG.RA FISHER	Piacere.
CRISTINA	Mi dispiace, sono in ritardo.
SIG.RA FISHER	Non importa. Come sta?
CRISTINA	Bene, grazie. E lei?
SIG.RA FISHER	Molto bene, grazie.

mi dispiace I'm sorry
sono in ritardo I'm late
non importa (literally it isn't important) it doesn't matter
come sta? how are you?
bene well; *molto bene* very well
E lei? and you?

9

CRISTINA	Lei è tedesca?
SIG.RA FISHER	No, sono inglese.
CRISTINA	Parla molto bene l'italiano!
SIG.RA FISHER	È molto gentile.
CRISTINA	Di dov'è? Di Londra?
SIG.RA FISHER	No, sono di Cambridge. E lei?
CRISTINA	Sono di Padova.

è tedesca? are you German (fem.)?
sono inglese I'm English (masc. and fem.)
parla molto bene l'italiano you speak Italian very well
è molto gentile you are very kind
di dov'è where are you from?
di Londra from London

HIRING A CAR

10

ZANETTI	Buongiorno.
IMPIEGATO	Buongiorno.
ZANETTI	Vorrei prenotare una macchina.
IMPIEGATO	Che tipo di macchina?
ZANETTI	Un'utilitaria.
IMPIEGATO	Va bene una . . . Fiat Panda?
ZANETTI	Va bene.
IMPIEGATO	Per quanto tempo?
ZANETTI	Una settimana.
IMPIEGATO	Che giorno le serve?
ZANETTI	Dal 26 maggio.
IMPIEGATO	Per sette giorni.
ZANETTI	Sì.
IMPIEGATO	Costa più o meno centomila lire al giorno.
ZANETTI	Va bene. Posso pagare con una carta di credito?
IMPIEGATO	Sì, può pagare con qualsiasi carta di credito: American Express, VISA, oppure la nostra carta di credito Hertz.
ZANETTI	Grazie.

vorrei prenotare una macchina I would like to reserve a car
che tipo di macchina? what kind of car?
un'utilitaria a small car
per quanto tempo? for how long?
una settimana a week
che giorno le serve? what day do you need it for?
dal 26 maggio from May 26
per sette giorni for seven days
più o meno more or less
al giorno per day
posso pagare con una carta di credito? may I pay with a credit card?

con qualsiasi carta di credito with any credit card
oppure or
la nostra carta our (credit) card

11

ZANETTI	Buongiorno. Ho prenotato una macchina.
IMPIEGATO	Buongiorno. A che nome?
ZANETTI	Zanetti.
IMPIEGATO	Ha la patente, per cortesia?
ZANETTI	Sì, eccola.
IMPIEGATO	Ha la carta di credito?
ZANETTI	Sì, la VISA.
IMPIEGATO	Molto bene.

ho prenotato una macchina I have reserved a car
a che nome? under what name?
ha la patente? have you got your driving license?

Exercise 4 ☆
You rent a car.

EXPLANATIONS

INTRODUCING YOURSELF

sono I am: *sono Zanetti* (literally I am Zanetti) my name is
Zanetti; *il nome è* the name is.

ADDRESSING PEOPLE

signor, signora, signorina
Signor is used without the article when addressing a man, and
is always followed by the surname: *signor Zanetti, signor
Borghesan*. So, *Buongiorno, signor Borghesan* Hello Mr.
Borghesan.

But, *vorrei parlare con **il** signor Borghesan* I'd like to speak to
Mr. Borghesan. *Signore* is only used without the surname
when addressing somebody you do not know: *scusi, signore?*
excuse me, sir?
Signora and *signorina* follow the same rule:
Buongiorno, signora Bianchi
Buonasera, signorina Degani but *ho un appuntamento con **la**
signora Bianchi, vorrei parlare con **la** signorina Degani.*
Note that *signorina*, although still common as a title and an
address, is used mainly with very young women.

INTRODUCING OTHER PEOPLE

Le presento May I introduce? *Le presento la mia collega* May I
introduce my colleague?

il direttore the managing director of a firm
la ditta the firm, the company
il direttore della vendite the marketing director
il vice-direttore the assistant manager
il titolare (masc.), *la titolare* (fem.) the owner of the firm
mio, mia my
la mia collega my colleague (fem.); *il mio collega* (masc.) *il mio
direttore*
To translate 'my' with words defining a close relative, drop *il,
la* etc:
mio marito my husband
mia moglie my wife
mio figlio my son
mia figlia my daughter

piacere (literally my pleasure) how do you do

BEING POLITE

come sta? how are you?   *sto bene* I am well
bene well   *e lei?* and you?

DI DOV'È?

di dov'è? where are you from?
sono di . . . I am from . . . *sono di Torino* I am from Turin; if
you want to say which country you come from, the easiest
way is to say that you are English, American, Italian, etc.:
sono inglese I am English

gallese Welsh	*francese* French
scozzese Scottish	*canadese* Canadian
irlandese Irish	

britannico (masc.), *britannica* (fem.) British
tedesco (masc.), *tedesca* (fem.) German
italiano (masc.), *italiana* (fem.) Italian
americano (masc.) *americana* (fem.) American
australiano (masc.) *australiana* (fem.) Australian

MAKING APPOINTMENTS

un appuntamento an appointment
fissare un appuntamento to make an appointment
vorrei fissare un appuntamento con . . . I'd like to make an
appointment with . . .
ho un appuntamento I have an appointment

USING THE PHONE

pronto? hello?
chi parla? who's speaking?
chi devo dire? who should I say?
come si chiama? what is your name? (literally how are you
called?)
il nome è . . . the name is . . .

Here are some answers you might get when you are trying to
contact somebody:
è occupato he is busy; *è occupata* she is busy

non è in sede he/she is not at the head office
non è in ufficio he/she is not in the office
è fuori he/she is out

la segreteria telefonica the answering machine (Note: *segretaria* is secretary.)
siamo temporaneamente assenti we are temporarily absent from the office

And here is what you might need to say:
sono occupato/a I am busy
ho un impegno I have a commitment
non posso I can't; *giovedì non posso* I can't make it on Thursday
può richiamarmi? can he/she call me back?; if you want to ask 'when can I call back?', you say *quando posso richiamare?*
quando torna? when does he/she get back?
mi dispiace, sono in ritardo I am sorry, I am late

THE ALPHABET

You will almost certainly have to spell your name when you are in Italy. The spelling in Italian is done using the names of cities, rather than of people or things, as in English: *R come Roma, M come Milano*, etc. Here is the complete list; listen to the tape for the pronunciation of the letters.

A	come Ancona	L	come Livorno
B	come Bologna	M	come Milano
C	come Como	N	come Napoli
D	come Domodossola	O	come Otranto
E	come Empoli	P	come Palermo
F	come Firenze	Q	come Quaderno (notebook)
G	come Genova	R	come Roma
H	come Hotel	S	come Savona
I	come Imola	T	come Torino
J	come Jersey	U	come Udine
K	come Kilo	V	come Venezia

W come Washington   Y come York
X ics   Z come Zurigo

WORTH KNOWING

TRAVELING BY CAR

Gasoline in Italy is sold by the liter, *al litro.* Ask for *il pieno* if
you want to fill the tank. If you want to save money you can
pay with coupons, which you can obtain from any branch
of the *Automobile Club d'Italia (ACI).* They will give you any
information relevant to your license, insurance, etc., in
connection with Italian law, and they will also carry out
emergency breakdown services on any roads.
gasoline is *benzina;* lead-free gas is *benzina senza piombo (verde*
green).

Motorways in Italy are *a pagamento* toll roads; you can get a
viacard, a credit card which you can use to pay *al casello* at the
tollbooth. It can be purchased from any ACI branch, but also
from service stations and even tobacconists. The symbol for
thruways is a black number, preceded by *A* for *Autostrada,* on a
green background.
Main roads are marked by the symbol *SS (strada statale* state
road); *tangenziale* or *circonvallazione* is the ring road:
tangenziale est east-bound ring road; *ovest* west; *nord* north; *sud*
south
If you want to rent a car, look for the sign *Autonoleggio* (car
rental) at the airport, or at the railway station. The categories of
cars vary from firm to firm, but if you want a small car, ask
for *un'utilitaria,* or for *un'economica.* You will be given *un
contratto* a contract, outlining the general agreement *(le
condizioni generali).* To rent a car you need to be 21, and 23 to
hire some of the most expensive, or biggest cars. The fee may
or may not include IVA *(Imposta sul valore aggiunto,* i.e. VAT).

CAN YOU GET BY?

Exercise 1 ☐☐
1 In answer to which of the following questions would you not give your name?
a   A che nome?
b   Come si chiama?
c   Chi parla?
d   Chi devo dire?
e   Come sta?

2 You are unlikely to go out for dinner with one of the following:
a   titolare
b   direttore
c   segreteria telefonica
d   segretaria

3 Which of the following would you not say when making an appointment?
a   Giovedì non posso.
b   Sono in ufficio domani.
c   Non è in sede.
d   Alle tre ho un impegno.

Exercise 2 ☆
You arrive late for an appointment.

Exercise 3 ☆☐☐
Listen to the recording of the Hertz employee summarizing the contract, and then fill in the details in the form provided opposite. (Transcript on page 112.)

AUTONOLEGGIO			
AUTO	N°GIORNI	DATA	TARIFFA
		DAL....AL....	£..........(IVA esclusa) £...........tutto incluso

Exercise 4 ☆
You receive a business call.

REFERENCE SECTION

PRONUNCIATION

The best way to develop a good pronunciation is to listen carefully to the dialogues on the cassettes, to repeat words and phrases, and to do the exercises until you are fluent. This brief guide only deals with the basics of Italian pronunciation.

Vowels in Italian are a little different from English ones; they are more 'open', and have fewer variations than the English ones:

A sounds like the 'u' in bunk: *banca, pasta*
E is like the 'e' in bet: *va bene, bicchiere*
I is like the 'ea' in tea: *vino*
O is like the 'o' in lot: *otto*
U is like the 'oo' in pool: *una*

Difficult sounds:
C followed by A, O, U or other consonants is a hard sound, as in cut, cat, etc: *cameriere, banca.*
C followed by E or I is soft, like 'ch' in church: *cento, arrivederci, cioccolata.*
CH is a hard sound: *pesche* (peaches)
G is also hard when followed by A, O, U: *albergo,* or by another consonant, *grande;* it is soft when followed by E or I: *Genova, giugno*
GH is a hard sound: *alberghi.*

GL is like 'lli' in million: *luglio, biglietto*.
GN is like 'ni' in onion: *signore, giugno, Gran Bretagna*.

H before a vowel is always mute: *ha, hanno* (pronounced A as the 'a' in *banca*).
QU is like 'qu' in quick: *quanto, quale*.
Z is either like the 'ts' in cats: *colazione*, or 'ds' as in lads: *zero, zucchero*.

STRESS

In many words, stress falls on the next-to-last syllable:
passaporto, biglietto, stazione, etc. but this is not always the case: *lettera, grazie, tavolo,* etc.
Words that end with an accented vowel must be pronounced with a strong stress on that vowel:
caffè, dov'è, città.

VERBS

Verbs in this course are taught as part of key phrases, and not by themselves, as you can get by without learning them properly. However, here are some basic ones, in all their forms, including the familiar *tu* forms which are not taught in this course:

to be	sono	I am
	sei	you are (familiar form)
	è	he/she/it is; you are (polite forms; *c'è* there is)
	siamo	we are
	siete	you are (plural)
	sono	they are (*ci sono* there are)

to have	ho	I have
	hai	you have (familiar form)
	ha	he/she/it has; you have (polite form)
	abbiamo	we have
	avete	you have (plural)
	hanno	they have

to speak	parlo	I speak
	parli	you speak (familiar form)
	parla	he/she speaks; you (polite) speak
	parliamo	we speak
	parlate	you (plural) speak
	parlano	they speak

Italian does not use the words for 'I,' 'you,' etc., very often because the verb forms indicate which person is doing what; you have come across *io* (I) and *lei,* you (polite form). The word for the familiar form of you is *tu.* It is used with family, friends, and people you call by their first name; it would be considered impolite to use it with anybody else, especially with people you have never met before.

NEGATIVES

To make the verb negative, you only need to put *non* in front of it: *non posso* I can't; *non mi piace* I don't like it; *non ho capito* I haven't understood.

NUMBERS

0	zero	11	undici	22	ventidue
1	uno	12	dodici	23	ventitré
2	due	13	tredici	24	ventiquattro

3	tre	14	quattordici	25	venticinque
4	quattro	15	quindici	26	ventisei
5	cinque	16	sedici	27	ventisette
6	sei	17	diciassette	28	ventotto
7	sette	18	diciotto	29	ventinove
8	otto	19	diciannove	30	trenta
9	nove	20	venti	31	trentuno
10	dieci	21	ventuno	32	trentadue
				33	trentatré
					etc.

40	quaranta	300	trecento
50	cinquanta	400	quattrocento
60	sessanta	500	cinquecento
70	settanta	600	seicento
80	ottanta	700	settecento
90	novanta	800	ottocento
100	cento	900	novecento
101	centoeuno	1000	mille
102	centodue	2000	duemila
200	duecento	10,000	diecimila
		100,000	centomila
		1,000,000	milione

LANGUAGE NOTES

Further and more detailed language notes can be found in the *Explanations* section of each unit.

Masculine and feminine	Unit 1

il and *la*	
del	
plurals	Unit 2
questo, questa	

TEMPERATURE CONVERSIONS

To change Fahrenheit to Centigrade, subtract 32 and multiply by $\frac{5}{9}$.
To change Centigrade to Fahrenheit, multiply by $\frac{9}{5}$ and add 32.

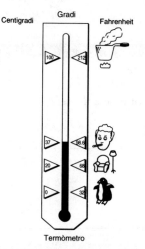

WEIGHTS AND MEASURES

Centimeters/Inches
It is usually unnecessary to make exact conversions from your customary inches to the metric system used in Italy, but to give you an approximate idea of how they compare, we give you the following guide.

To convert **centimetri** into inches, multiply by .39.

To convert inches into **centimetri,** multiply by 2.54.

Centimetri

Pollici

Meters / Feet
1 meter **(metro)** = 39.37 inches
            = 3.28 feet
            = 1.09 yards

1 foot = 0.3 meters
1 yard = 0.9 meters

Kilograms / Pounds
1 kilogram **(chilo)** = 2.2 pounds
1 pound   = 0.45 kilogram

Liters / Quarts
1 liter = 1.06 quarts
4 liters = 1.06 gallons

For quick approximate conversion, multiply the number of gallons by 4 to get liters **(litri).** Divide the number of liters by 4 to get gallons.

IMPORTANT SIGNS

Acqua (non)potabile	(Not) potable water
Alt	Stop
Aperto	Open
Attenzione	Caution, watch out
Avanti	Enter (come in, go, walk [at the lights])
Caldo or "C"	Hot
Chiuso	Closed
Divieto di sosta	No parking
Divieto di transito	No entrance, keep out
Freddo or "F"	Cold
Gabinetti (WC)	Toilets
Ingresso	Entrance
Libero	Vacant
Non toccare	Hands off, don't touch
Occupato	Occupied
Pericolo	Danger
Riservato	Reserved
Si vende	For sale
Signora	Women's room
Signore	Men's room
Spingere	Push
Tirare	Pull
Uscita	Exit
Vietato fumare	No smoking

ROAD SIGNS

Guarded railroad crossing

Yield

Stop

Right of way

Dangerous intersection ahead

Gasoline (petrol) ahead

Parking

No vehicles allowed

Dangerous curve

Pedestrian crossing

Oncoming traffic has right of way

No bicycles allowed

No parking allowed

No entry

No left turn

No U-turn

No passing

Border crossing

Traffic signal ahead

Speed limit

Traffic circle (roundabout) ahead

Minimum speed limit

All traffic turns left

End of no passing zone

One-way street

Detour

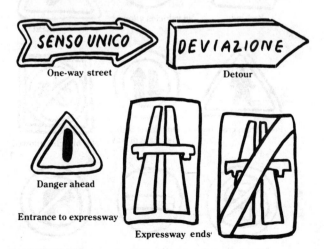
Danger ahead

Entrance to expressway

Expressway ends

MENU ITEMS

Appetizers (Starters)

Antipasti mostly consist of raw salads, cooked chilled vegetables dressed with a vinaigrette, and massive varieties of sausages and salamis. Some key terms are:

acciughe	*ah-chee-OH-gheh*	anchovies
antipasto misto	*ahn-tee-pAHs-toh mEEs-toh*	assorted appetizers
carciofi	*kahr-chee-OH-fee*	artichoke
mortadella	*mohr-tah-dEHl-lah*	cold sausage, similar to bologna
prosciutto crudo	*proh-shee-OOt-toh krOO-doh*	raw cured ham
tartufi	*tahr-tOO-fee*	truffles (white)

Soups

Soups can be either thick or thin, and thus are given different names. **Brodi** are generally broths, while **zuppe** are thick and hearty.

brodo di manzo	*brOH-doh dee mAHn-tsoh*	broth, generally meat-based
brodo di pollo	*brOH-hod dee pOHl-loh*	chicken broth
brodo magro di vegetali	*brOH-doh mAH-groh dee veh-jeh-tAH-lee*	vegetable broth
crema di ____	*krEH-mah dee*	creamed ____ soup
cacciucco	*kah-chee-OO-koh*	seafood chowder
minestra in brodo	*mee-nEHs-trah een brOH-doh*	pasta in broth
minestrone	*mee-nehs-trOH-neh*	thick vegetable soup
zuppa di ____	*tsOOp-pah dee*	thick soup

Entrees (Meat and Fish Dishes)
The "main course" of an Italian meal is usually either a sautéed
or grilled meat or a baked fish or chicken. Along the coast
you'll find unusual varieties of seafood.

acciughe	*ah-chee-OO-gheh*	anchovies
anguille	*ahn-goo-EEl-leh*	eel
aragosta	*ah-rah-gOHs-tah*	lobster (spiny)
baccalà	*bah-kah-lAH*	dried salt cod
branzino	*brahn-tsEE-noh*	bass (hake)
(nasello)	*(nah-sEHl-loh)*	
calamari (seppie)	*kah-lah-mAH-ree*	squid
	(sAYp-pee-eh)	
cozze	*kOH-tseh*	mussels
gamberetti	*gAHm-beh-rAY-tee*	prawns
granchi	*grAHn-key*	crabs
lumache	*loo-mAH-keh*	snails
merluzzo	*mayr-lOOt-tsoh*	cod
ostriche	*OHs-tree-keh*	oysters
polipo	*pOH-lee-poh*	octopus
salmone	*sahl-mOH-neh*	salmon
sardine	*sahr-dEE-neh*	sardines
scampi	*skAHm-pee*	shrimps
sogliola	*sOH-ly-ee-oh-lah*	flounder (sole)
trota	*trOH-tah*	trout
tonno	*tOHn-noh*	tuna
vongole	*vOHn-goh-leh*	clams
trance di pesce alla griglia	*trAHn-chee dee pAY-sheh AHl-lah grEE-ly-ee-ah*	grilled fish steaks
fritto misto di pesce	*frEEt-toh mEEs-toh dee pAY-sheh*	mixed fried fish

Meat dishes are often sauced or served with gravy.

agnello	*ah-ny-EHl-loh*	lamb
(abbacchio)	*(ahb-bAH-key-oh)*	
capretto	*kah-prAYy-toh*	goat
maiale	*mah-ee-AH-leh*	pork
manzo	*mAHn-tsoh*	beef
montone	*mohn-tOH-neh*	mutton
vitello	*vee-tEHl-loh*	veal

Some common cuts of meat, plus other menu terms:

affettati	*ahf-fayt-tAH-tee*	cold cuts
anitra	*AH-nee-trah*	duck
costate	*kohs-tAH-teh*	chops
animelle	*ah-nee-mEHl-leh*	sweetbreads
cervello	*chehr-vEHl-loh*	brains
fegato	*fAY-gah-toh*	liver
bistecca	*bees-tAY-kah*	steak
lingua	*lEEn-goo-ah*	tongue
pancetta	*pahn-chAYt-tah*	bacon
pollo	*pOHl-loh*	chicken
polpette	*pohl-pAYt-teh*	meatballs
prosciutto	*proh-shee-OOt-toh*	ham
rognoni	*roh-ny-OH-nee*	kidneys
tacchino	*tah-kEY-noh*	turkey

Vegetables

asparagi	*ahs-pAH-rah-jee*	asparagus
carciofi	*kahr-chee-OH-fee*	artichoke
carote	*kah-rOH-teh*	carrots
cavoli	*kAH-voh-lee*	cabbage
cavolfiori	*kah-vohl-fee-OH-ree*	cauliflower

cetriolo	*cheh-tree-OO-loh*	cucumber
ceci	*chay-chee*	chick-peas
fagioli	*fah-jee-oh-lEE*	beans (dried)
fagiolini	*fah-jee-oh-lEE-nee*	green beans
funghi	*fOOn-ghee*	mushrooms
lattuga	*laht-tOO-gah*	lettuce
lenticchie	*len-tEE-key-eh*	lentils
melanzana	*meh-lAHn-tsah-nah*	eggplant
peperoni	*peh-peh-rOH-nee*	pepper
patate	*pah-tAH-teh*	potatoes
piselli	*pee-sEHl-lee*	peas
pomodoro	*poh-moh-dOH-roh*	tomato
porcini	*pohr-chee-nee*	wild mushroom
sedano	*sAY-dah-noh*	celery
spinaci	*spee-nAH-chee*	spinach

Fruits

albicocca	*ahl-bee-kOH-kah*	apricot
ananasso	*ah-nah-nAHs-soh*	pineapple
arancia	*ah-rAHn-chee-ah*	orange
ciliege	*chee-lee-EH-jee-eh*	cherries
fragole	*frAH-goh-leh*	strawberries
lampone	*lahm-pOH-neh*	raspberry
limone	*lee-mOH-neh*	lemon
mela	*mAY-lah*	apple
melone	*meh-LOH-neh*	melon
pera	*pAY-rah*	pear
pesca	*pAYS-kah*	peach
pompelmo	*pohm-pEHl-moh*	grapefruit
prugne	*prOO-ny-eh*	plum
uva	*OO-vah*	grape

KEY TO EXERCISES

1 SAYING HELLO AND ORDERING DRINKS

Exercise 1

Transcript:

SERGIO	Allora . . . due più tre . . .	2+3
DAUGHTER	Cinque.	5
SERGIO	Tre più tre . . .	3+3
DAUGHTER	Sei.	6
SERGIO	Dieci meno cinque . . .	10−5
DAUGHTER	Cinque.	5
SERGIO	Cinque più tre . . .	5+3
DAUGHTER	Otto.	8
SERGIO	Otto più due . . .	8+2
DAUGHTER	Dieci.	10
SERGIO	Due . . . più quattro . . .	2+4
DAUGHTER	Sei.	6
SERGIO	Nove più uno . . .	9+1
DAUGHTER	Dieci.	10
SERGIO	Uno più uno . . .	1+1
DAUGHTER	Due.	2

Exercise 2

Transcript:

a Il telefono è nove nove zero zero zero uno zero (9900010).

b Se vuole il numero di telefono? Allora, cinque due
nove uno uno zero otto (5291108).

c Il numero di telefono? Allora: otto due zero nove sette
undici (8209711).

Exercise 4
Transcript:

MICHELE	Eh . . . il Brachetto è un vino bianco o rosso?
CAMERIERE	Il Brachetto è un vino rosso dolce.
MICHELE	Ah, bene. Allora, due bicchieri di Brachetto e . . . vino bianco secco?
CAMERIERE	Vino bianco secco . . . potrei darle del Soave.
MICHELE	Bene. Allora, due bicchieri di Brachetto e tre bicchieri di Soave.

VINO	BIANCO	ROSSO	DOLCE	SECCO
Brachetto		✓	✓	
Soave	✓			✓

CAN YOU GET BY?

Exercise 1 Word search

```
U  E  B  S  T  E  I  Z  A  R  G  O  M  P
L  N  U  A  R  P  C  C  D  F  H  A  N  Y
B  U  O  N  G  I  O  R  N  O  A  L  E  S
L  O  N  A  D  F  E  L  P  Q  S  U  I  T
O  L  A  R  T  D  D  S  O  A  F  I  L  R
R  I  S  T  O  P  E  R  F  A  V  O  R  E
Q  P  E  A  N  R  V  O  E  B  B  C  D  I
A  P  R  E  G  O  I  D  Z  Z  F  P  N  U
L  A  A  E  R  I  R  D  O  Z  P  S  V  V
V  L  Z  P  D  R  R  I  A  A  E  Q  P  Q
V  U  E  E  L  O  A  I  C  R  S  V  Z  H
```

Exercise 2
Bingo card, 600 *seicento* has
not been called.

Exercise 3
1b, 2b, 3c, 4a, 5b

2 SHOPPING

Exercise 3
Transcript: Abbiamo: eh . . . fragola, limone, pistacchio,
pesca, pera, pompelmo, mirtillo, ananas. Poi abbiamo:
stracciatella, nocciola, cioccolato, yogurt, tiramisù, panna e
vaniglia.
Translation: We have: strawberry, lemon, pistachio, peach, pear,
grapefruit, blueberry, pineapple. Then we have: chocolate
chip, hazelnut, chocolate, yogurt, *tiramisù* (lit., pick-me-up, a
Venetian sweet), cream and vanilla.
Key: yes, he does: pesca and cioccolato.

CAN YOU GET BY?

Exercise 2
Transcript: Tremilasettecentocinquanta 3,750 lire
Ottomila lire 8,000 lire
Quattromilanovecinquanta 4,950
Trentamila 30,000
Ventiduemiladuecento lire 22,200 lire.

Exercise 3
1b, 2b, 3c, 4c, 5b

3 TRAVELING AROUND

Exercise 2
a   Un'andata per Roma, per favore

b Due biglietti di andate e ritorno per Napoli in prima classe
c Venezia, andata e ritorno, con supplemento rapido

Exercise 3
Le cinque e mezza 5:30
mezzogiorno meno un quarto 11:45
l'una e dieci 1:10
le dodici e venti 12:20
le diciotto e quaranta 18:40 (6:40)
mezzanotte meno cinque 11:55

Exercise 4
Timetable: the train leaves Milan at 7:55; it arrives at Bologna at 9:42; the connection is at 10:00; it arrives in Florence at 10:46.

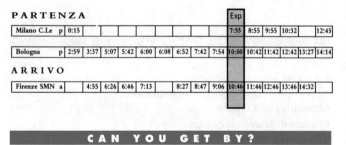

IL RITORNO DA **MILANO-BOLOGNA** PER **FIRENZE**

PARTENZA

									Exp					
Milano C.Le p	0:15									7:55	8:55	9:55	10:32		12:45

Bologna p	2:59	3:37	5:07	5:42	6:00	6:08	6:52	7:42	7:54	10:00	10:42	11:42	12:42	13:27	14:14

ARRIVO

Firenze SMN a		4:55	6:26	6:46	7:13		8:27	8:47	9:06	10:46	11:46	12:46	13:46	14:32	

CAN YOU GET BY?

Exercise 1
Transcript: Allora, di mattina dalle nove alle dodici e trenta . . . dalle nove alle dodici e trenta. E di pomeriggio, dalle quattordici alle diciannove . . . dalle quattordici alle diciannove.
Key: From 14:00 till 19:00.

Exercise 2
1b, 2c, 3b, 4c

4 GETTING SOMEWHERE TO STAY

Exercise 3
Transcript: Una camera doppia costa centoeunmila lire, esclusa la colazione. Eh, la colazione costa tredicimila lire a persona. Eh, una camera singola costa sessantottomila lire, esclusa la colazione, e . . . tutte le camere hanno i servizi e la doccia. Le camere matrimoniali hanno la vasca da bagno e costano centoeottomila lire, esclusa la colazione.
Key: 101,000 lire + 13,000 + 13,000 = 127,000

Exercise 4
Transcript: due ragazzi e una ragazza; un ragazzo e tre ragazze; tre ragazze e quattro ragazzi; quattro ragazze e due ragazzi.

26 MAGGIO	RAGAZZI	RAGAZZE
	2	1
	1	3
	4	3
	2	4

Exercise 6
Transcript: Da gennaio a febbraio, sono a Londra . . .
Da marzo a luglio, sono a Roma per un film . . .
Da agosto a settembre, sono a Venezia . . .
In ottobre, vado in America per due mesi . . .
Torno a Londra in dicembre . . .

CAN YOU GET BY?

Exercise 1
Transcript: Trenta giorni ha novembre, con aprile, giugno e settembre; di ventotto ce n'è uno (febbraio); tutti gli altri ne han trentuno.

Translation: Thirty days hath November, with April, June and September; there's one with twenty eight (days) (February); all the others have thirty one (days).

5 EATING OUT

Exercise 2
Transcript: Come primo piatto abbiamo; delle pappardelle, agli asparagi freschi. Abbiamo una zuppa, agli asparagi. Ci sono i gnocchi di patate, alle salse; i bigoli – sono gli spaghetti grossi, fatti in casa, alle salse. Ci sono i risotti, agli asparagi, all'ortica, alla quaglia . . .

Translation: As first course we have: *pappardelle* (a type of pasta) with fresh asparagus sauce. We have a soup, of asparagus. There are potato *gnocchi* with a choice of different sauces; *bigoli* – they're the thick, home-made spaghetti, with different sauces. There are risottos with asparagus, nettles, quail . . .

CAN YOU GET BY?

Exercise 1
Here is the solved puzzle.

	²P		⁶V		³C		⁴M			⁵D
¹V	E	G	E	T	A	R	I	A	N	O
	S		R		R		P			L
	C		D		N		I			C
	E		U		E		A			E
			R				C			
			E				E			

Exercise 2
a forno, **b** cameriere, **c** tagliata di manzo, **d** Le piace la sua braciola di vitello? **e** torta alla ricotta

6 MEETING PEOPLE AND DOING BUSINESS

Exercise 2
Transcript: La signora Rossi è libera martedì alle undici, mercoledì alle sedici e trenta e giovedì alle quindici e trenta. Quando le va bene?
Key: Giovedì alle quindici e trenta (Thursday at 15:30).

Exercise 3
Translation: Buongiorno. Sono Vivian Stewart. Sono la titolare della ditta Stewart Software. Vorrei fissare un appuntamento con il direttore delle vendite. Può richiamarmi? Il mio numero è zero due . . . tre uno . . . otto uno . . . otto due . . . sette cinque. Sono in ufficio domani mattina. Grazie, buongiorno.

CAN YOU GET BY?

Exercise 1
1e, 2c, 3c

Exercise 3
Transcript: Ecco. Questo è il contratto. Lei ha noleggiato una macchina dal 15 di agosto fino al 30 di agosto, per quindici giorni, a centomila lire al giorno; è una Fiat Uno, tutto incluso.

Translation: Here (it is). This is the contract. You have rented a car from August 15 to August 30, for fifteen days, at 100,000 lire per day; it's a Fiat Uno, everything included.

A U T O N O L E G G I O			
AUTO	N°GIORNI	DATA	TARIFFA
Fiat Uno	15	DAL15/8	£............(IVA esclusa)
		AL 30/8	£100,000 tutto incluso

WORD LIST

ITALIAN-ENGLISH

All translations given are as used in this book. Bold type
shows where the stress falls in each word.
Abbreviations: M. = masculine, f. = feminine, sing. =
singular, pl. = plural.
Adjectives are listed with their masculine and feminine endings
(freddo, -a) . . .

A

a   at, to
*abbi**a**mo*   we have
ac***como***di: s'ac***como***di   please go to, please sit down
l'   ***ac***qua (f.)   water.
l'   ***ac***qua mine***ra***le   mineral water; *l'**ac**qua mine**ra**le
   gas***sa***ta (or *friz**zan**te*)   sparkling mineral water; *l'**ac**qua
   mine**ra**le non gas**sa**ta (or *natu**ra**le*)   regular mineral water
l'   a***dul***to (m.)   adult
l'   ***ag***lio (m.)   garlic
   ai (= a + i)   at/to the
   *ai **fun**ghi*   with mushrooms
   al (= a + il)   at/to the; *al **lat**te/li**mo**ne*   with milk/lemon;
   *al se**ma**foro*   at the lights; *al **ton**no*   with tuna fish sauce
l'   al***ber***go   hotel; *l'alberga**to**re* (m.), *l'albergatri**ce***

(f.)   hotelier
all' (= a + l')
alla (= a + la)   at/to the, in the style of . . . : *alla*
   quaglia   with quail; *alla vicentina*   in the style of
   Vicenza
alle (= a + le) (+ time)   at . . .
allora   now then
americano, -a   American
anche   too, also
andare   to go: *per andare a . . . ?* the way to . . . ?
andata   one-way: *andata e ritorno* round-trip
l' *anitra* (f.)   duck
l' *antipasto* (m.)   starter
aperto, -a   open
appetito   appetite: *buon appetito*   bon appetit
l' *appuntamento* (m.)   appointment
arance   oranges
l' *aranciata* (f.)   orangeade
l' *aria condizionata* (f.)   air conditioning
arrivederci   goodbye
l' *arrivo* (m.)   arrival
l' *ascensore* (m.)   lift
assenti (pl.)   absent
australiano, -a   Australian
l' *autobus* (m.)   bus
l' *autonoleggio* (m.)   car rental/lease
l' *autostrada* (f.)   thruway
avete   do you (pl.) have?

B

il **bagno**   bath
il **bambino**   child
la **banca**   bank
il **bar**   bar

basta enough: **basta così?** is that enough? is that all?
basta, grazie that's all, thanks
bene well: *va bene* OK, fine; *benissimo* very well,
very good
la **benzina** gasoline
bere to drink: *qualcosa da bere* something to drink
bianco, -a white
il **bicchiere** glass
la **biglietteria** ticket office
il **biglietto** ticket
il **binario** platform
la **birra** beer
la **bistecca** steak
la **borsetta** handbag
la **bottiglia** bottle
la **braciola** chop
la **brioche** bun
britannico, -a British
buonanotte goodnight
buonasera hello, good evening
buongiorno hello, good morning
buonissimo, -a excellent
buono, -a good
il **burro** butter

C

il **caffè** coffee: *il caffè lungo* weaker black coffee; *il
caffè macchiato* coffee with a dash of milk
cambiare to change: **posso cambiare . . . ?** can I
change . . . ?
il **cambio** exchange
la **camera** bedroom
il **campeggio** campsite
canadese (m. and f.) Canadian

la cantina   wine shop
  capito   understood: *non ho capito*   I didn't
    understand
il cappuccino   espresso with steamed milk
la carne   meat
  caro, -a   expensive
la carta di credito   credit card
la carta telefonica   phone card
la cartolina   postcard
la cassa   till, till counter
  c'è   there is
il centro   centre: *il centro città*   city center
  certo   certainly
  che   that, what, which? *a che ore?*   at what time? *da che
    binario?*   from which platform?
  chi?   who? *chi devo dire?*   who shall I say?
la chiave   key
il chilo   kilo
  chiuso, -a   closed
  ciao   hello, hi, bye
la cipolla   onion
la città   city, town
la classe   class: *prima classe*   first class
la coincidenza   connection
la colazione   breakfast
il/ la collega   colleague
  come   as, like: *come primo*   as first course; *come si
    chiama?*   what is your name? (polite form); *come
    sta?*   how are you? (polite form)
  completo: al completo   fully booked
  con   with
  continua   you continue: *continua sempre dritto*   you
    continue straight on (polite form)
il conto   bill
il contorno   vegetables or salad (side dish)

il *contratto* contract

corrente: la presa di corrente electrical outlet

cosa what: *cosa prendono?* what will you have?;

cos'è? what is (it)?

costa it costs: *quanto costa?* how much does it cost?

cotto, -a cooked

crudo, -a raw; cured: *prosciutto crudo* cured ham (e.g.,
  Parma)

D

da from: *da bere* to drink; *d'accordo* agreed, OK; *da
  cinquemila* five thousand (lire) worth

dal (= da + il) *binario quattro* from platform (number)
  four

dalle (da + le) *due* from 2 o'clock

dei (= di + i) any, some: *dei gettoni* any, some telephone
  tokens

del (di + il) any, some: *ha del formaggio?* do you have
  any cheese?

desidera? may I help you?

la *destinazione* destination

destra right: *a destra* to the right; *sulla destra* on the
  right

di of

la *diarrea* diarrhea

il *diretto* train that has designated stops

il *direttore* the managing director: *il direttore delle vendite*
  the marketing director

dispiace: mi dispiace I'm sorry

la *doccia* shower

il *documento* document

il *dolce* dessert

il *dollaro* dollar

domani tomorrow

domenica Sunday
dopo after
dopodomani the day after tomorrow
doppia: camera doppia twin-bedded room
dove? where? *dov'è?* where is?
dritto straight on
il *duomo* cathedral

E

e and
è is
ecco here is . . . : *ecco il caffè* here is the coffee; *èccoli*
   here they are
esclusa: IVA esclusa VAT excluded
l' *espresso* (m.) small black coffee
etto 100 grams

F

fagioli beans
fagiolini string beans
la *farmacia* pharmacy
le *ferie* holiday
   chiuso per ferie closed for vacation
la *fermata* bus stop
la *fiera* trade fair
il *filetto* fillet
   fino as far as, to, until: *fino al semaforo* as far as the (traffic)
     light; *fino alle due* until 2 o'clock
   firmare to sign: *può firmare?* can you sign?
   fissare to arrange
il *formaggio* cheese
il *forno* oven: *al forno* oven-heated
la *fragola* strawberry

francese (m. and f.) French
il *francobollo* stamp
   fritto, -a fried
la *frutta* fruit
il *fruttivendolo* fruitseller
   fumatori: fumatori o non fumatori? smoking or non-smoking?
   funghi mushrooms
   fuori out, outside: *fuori della stazione* outside the station

G

gallese (m. and f.) Welsh
   gassata: acqua minerale gassata sparkling mineral water
il *gelato* ice cream
   gentile kind: *è molto gentile* you (polite form) are very kind
il *gettone* telephone token
il *giorno* day: *al giorno* per day
il *giovedì* Thursday
   giri turn: *giri a sinistra* turn left
   giusto? is that right?
le *gocce* drops (medicinal)
la *Gran Bretagna* Great Britain
   grazie thank you
il *gusto* flavor

H

ha he/she has; you have (polite form): *ha del formaggio?* do you have any cheese?
ho I have: *non ho capito* I didn't understand

I   the (m. pl.)
ieri   yesterday
il   the (m. sing.)
l' impegno (m.)   commitment
l' impiegato (m.)   employee
importa: non importa   it doesn't matter
in   in
incluso   included: *tutto incluso*   everything included
informazioni   (pl.) information: *informazioni turistiche*
   tourist information
l' Inghilterra (f.)   England
l' insalata (f.)   salad
invece   instead
io   I
irlandese (m. and f.)   Irish
italiano, -a   Italian

l'   the (sing.)
la   the (f. sing.)
là   there
lascia: mi lascia il suo numero?   will you leave me your
   number?
il latte   milk: *al latte*   with milk
le   the (f. pl.)
le   you, to you: *le piace?*   do you like it?
la lettera   letter
il letto   bed: *una camera a due letti*   a twin room
libero, -a   free
la limonata   lemonade
il limone   lemon
la linea   telephone line: *rimanga in linea*   hold the line

la **li***ra*   lira
il **lo***cale*   a train stopping at all stations
il **lun***edì*   Monday

M

la **ma***cchina*   car
la **ma***celleria*   butcher's shop
il **ma***iale*   pork
   mal: mal di denti   toothache; *mal di stomaco*   stomachache
la **man***cia*   tip
   mangiare   to eat
il **man***zo*   beef
   margherita: la pizza margherita   pizza with tomato sauce
      and mozzarella cheese
il **mar***ito*   husband
il **mar***tedì*   Tuesday
   matrimoniale   a room with a double bed
   massimo   maximum: *al massimo di*   for a maximum of
   me   me: *per me*   for me
il **mel***one*   melon
   meno   less
il **men***ù*   menu
il **mer***cato*   market; *il supermercato*   supermarket
   mezzanotte   midnight
   mezzo   half: *mezzo chilo*   half a kilo
   mezzogiorno   midday
   mi   me, to me: *mi dispiace*   I'm sorry; *mi piace*   I like; *mi
   lascia il suo numero?*   will you leave me your number?
   mi*la*   thousand(s)
   mi*lle*   a thousand
   minerale   mineral
   mio   my, mine (m. sing.)
   misto, -a   mixed
   molto   very

N

il/ la *negoziante*   shopkeeper
   niente   nothing, no: *niente dolce, grazie*   no dessert, thank
     you
   no   no
   noi   we, us
   noleggiato   hired: *ho noleggiato*   I have hired
il *nome*   name
   non   not
la *notte*   night
il *numero*   number: *il numero undici*   (room) number eleven

O

   occupato   busy: *è occupato*   he's busy
   oggi   today
l' *olio* (m.)   oil (olive): *all'olio*   with olive oil
l' *ombra*   shade: *all'ombra*   in the shade
   oppure   or
   ora   hour, time: *a che ora?*   at what time?; *che ore sono*
     what time is it?
l' *orario* (m.)   timetable, schedule, opening hours
l' *ostello* (m.)   hostel: *l'ostello della gioventù*   youth hostel
   ottimo   excellent

P

il *pacchettino*   airmail parcel: *le faccio un pacchettino?*   shall I
   gift-wrap it?
il *pacchetto*   package, parcel
il *panino*   bread roll
   parlare   to speak
il *parmigiano*   parmesan cheese
   parte   it leaves: *a che ora parte?*   at what time does it leave?

la partenza departure
il passaporto passport
la pasta pasta, cake
la pasticceria patisserie
la patente driving license
la pensione small hotel: *mezza pensione* half-board;
  pensione completa full board
  per for, to: *per cortesia/per favore* please; *per me* for me;
    per Vicenza to Vicenza
  permesso excuse me, may I come past/come in?
  però but
la persona person
la pesca peach
il pesce fish
il pezzo piece: *un pezzo di formaggio* a piece of cheese
  piace: le piace? do you like it?
  piacere how do you do?
il piano floor: *il primo piano* first floor
la pianta map
il piatto dish: *piatti (pl.) del giorno* dishes of the day
  piccante spicy
  piccolo, -a small, little
il piombo lead: *senza piombo* lead-free
la piscina swimming pool
  più more, plus
la pizza pizza
la pizzeria pizzeria
  po': un po' a little, *un po' di . . .* a little (of)
  poi then, anything else?
il pollo chicken
il pomeriggio afternoon
il pomodoro tomato: *al pomodoro* with tomato
il pompelmo grapefruit
il portafoglio wallet
  porta: ci porta? (will) you bring us?

*po*sso? can, may I?

il *po*sto place, room: *c'è posto?* is there room?

il *pran*zo lunch, main meal

*prefe*risco I prefer

*pre*go don't mention it, may I help you?

*pren*do I'll have: *prendono* they'll have

*preno*tato reserved: *ho prenotato* I have reserved

la *preno*tazi*o*ne booking, reservation

il *pre*zzo price

il *pri*mo the first: *il primo (piatto)* the first course; *il primo piano* the first floor

la *presa di corren*te electrical outlet

*presen*to: *le presento la mia collega?* (may) I introduce my colleague?

la *profu*me*ri*a perfume shop

*pron*to here is: *pronto/i il caffè* here is the coffee

*pron*to? hello?

il *prosciu*tto ham

*pro*ssimo, -a next

*pu*ò can he/she/you (polite form): *può firmare?* can you sign?

la *qua*glia quail

*qualco*sa something: *qualcosa da bere* something to drink

*qua*le? which one?

*qual*siasi any

*quan*do? when?

*quan*ti? how many?

*quan*to? how much?: *quanto costa?* how much does it cost?; *quant'è?* how much is it?; *quanto viene?* how much does it come to?

*quar*to: *un quarto* a quarter: *le due e un quarto* a quarter past two

questo, -a   this, this one
qui   here
quindi   then

R

il *raffreddore*   a cold
la *ragazza*   girl
il *ragazzo*   boy
il *rapido*   fast train
regionale   typical of a region
il *resto*   the change
richiamare   to call back
ripetere   to repeat
il *riso*   rice
il *risotto*   risotto
il *ristorante*   restaurant
il *ritardo*   delay: *in ritardo*   late; *sono in ritardo*   I'm late
il *ritorno*   return
rosso, -a   red
la *rosticceria*   a take-out establishment specializing in roast meats
la *roulotte*   caravan

S

sai: sai dire?   can you say?
salato, -a   savory, salty
il *salmone*   salmon
la *salsa*   sauce
la *salumeria*   cooked meats shop
scozzese (m. and f.)   Scottish
scusi?   excuse me?
il *secondo*   (the) second; the second course
la *sede*   the main office, head office
la *segretaria*   secretary

la segreteria telefonica   the answering machine
il semaforo   the lights
    sempre   always, still: *sempre dritto*   straight ahead
    senza   without
le seppie (pl.)   cuttlefish
la sera   evening
il servizio in camera   room service: *il servizio sveglia*   wake-up
    service
    servono: mi servono i passaporti   I need your passports
    sì   yes
    siamo   we are
il signor . . .   Mr . . .
la signora   lady, Mrs . . .
il signore   gentleman
la signorina   Miss . . . , young lady
    singola   single
    sinistra   left: *a sinistra*   to the left
    soltanto   only
    sono   I am
    specialità   a typical dish
le stagioni   seasons
    stamattina   this morning
la stanza   bedroom
la stazione   railway station
la sterlina   pound sterling
    storico, -a   historic
la strada   road
    subito   immediately
il suo   his/her/s; your/yours (polite)
il supermercato   supermarket
il supplemento   supplement

T

il *tabaccaio*   tobacconist
la *tavola calda*   self-service restaurant
il *tè*   tea
   tedesco, -a   German
il *telefono*   telephone
la *televisione*   television; TV set
   temporaneamente   temporarily
la *tenda*   tent
la *terrazza*   balcony
il *tipo*   type
il/ la *titolare*   the owner (of the firm)
la *toilette*   toilet
il *tonno*   tuna fish
   torna   he, she comes back: *quando torna?*   when does he
      come back?
la *torta*   cake, sweet
   tra   between, within: *tra un'ora*   in an hour's time
la *trattoria*   small family restaurant
   troppo   too, too much
la *trota*   trout
   trovare   to find
il *turno: chiuso per turno*   weekly closing day

U

l' *ufficio* (m.)   office: *in ufficio*   in the office; *l'ufficio postale*
      post office
   un'   a, an (f. sing.)
   un   a, an (m. sing.)
   una   a, an (f. sing.)
l' *utilitaria*   small car

V

vada   go: *vada dritto*   go straight on
la *valigeria*   leather-goods shop
vede   you (polite form) see
vegetariano, -a   vegetarian
verde   green
verdura   vegetables
verso   at around, toward: *versi le tre*   at around 3 o'clock
il *viaggio*   journey trip
il *vice-direttore*   assistant manager
vicino, -a   near
il *vino*   wine
il *vitello*   veal
volte: tre volte al giorno   three times a day
vorrei   I would like
il *vostro: il vostro vino della casa*   your house wine
vuole?   would you like?

Z

la *zuppa*   soup
lo *zucchero*   sugar

ENGLISH-ITALIAN

A

a, an   un, uno (m.);   un', una (f.)
absent   assenti (pl.)
adult   l'adulto (m.)
after   dopo
afternoon   il pomeriggio
agreed, OK   d'accordo
air conditioning   l'aria condizionata (f.)
airmail parcel   il pacchettino
also   anche
always, still   sempre; *straight ahead*   sempre dritto
American   americano, -a
and   e
answering machine   la segreteri telefonica
any   qualsiasi
anything else?   poi?
appetite   appetito; *bon appetit*   buon appetito
appetizer   l'antipasto (m.)
appointment   l'appuntamento (m.)
to arrange   fissare
arrival   l'arrivo (m.)
as far as, to, until   fino; *as far as the lights*   fino al semaforo;
   until two o'clock   fino alle due
as, like   come; *as a first course*   come primo
assistant manager   il vice-direttore
at, to   a
Australian   australiano, -a

B

balcony   la terrazza
bank   la banca

bar   il bar
bath   il **ba**gno
beans   fagi**o**li
bed   il **le**tto; *a twin-bedded room*   una c**a**mera a d**u**e **le**tti
bedroom   la c**a**mera, la st**a**nza
beef   il m**a**nzo
beer   la **bi**rra
between, within   tra; *within an hour*   tra un'**o**ra
bill   il c**o**nto
bottle   la bott**i**glia
boy   il rag**a**zzo
breakfast   la colazi**o**ne
bring: (will) you bring us?   ci p**o**rta?
British   brit**a**nnico, -a
bun   la bri**o**che
bus   l'**au**tobus (m.)
bus stop   la ferm**a**ta
busy   occup**a**to; *he's busy*   è occup**a**to
but   per**ò**
butcher shop   la macelle**r**ia
butter   il **bu**rro

C

---

cake   la t**o**rta
to call back   richiam**a**re
campsite   il camp**e**ggio
can: he/she/you can (polite)   pu**ò**; *can you sign?*   pu**ò** firm**a**re?;
   can you say? (informal)   s**a**i d**i**re?; *can, may I?*   p**o**sso?
Canadian   cana**de**se (m. and f.)
car   la m**a**cchina; *car rental/lease*   l'autono**leg**gio (m.); *small car*
   l'utilit**a**ria
caravan   la roul**o**tte
cashier's counter   la **ca**ssa
cathedral   il du**o**mo

center   il c**en**tro; *city center*   il c**en**tro città
certainly   c**er**to
to change   cambi**a**re; *can I change. . . ?*   **po**sso cambi**a**re. . . ?
change   *(money)*   il r**e**sto
cheese   il form**a**ggio
chicken   il p**o**llo
child   il bam**bi**no
chop   la braci**o**la
city, town   la citt**à**
class   la cl**a**sse; *first class*   **pri**ma classe
closed   chi**u**so, -a; *holiday closing*   il chi**u**so per f**e**rie; *weekly
   closing*   il chiuso per turno
coffee   il caff**è**: *weaker black coffee*   il caff**è** l**un**go; *coffee with a
   dash of milk*   il caff**è** macchiato; *small black coffee*   l'esp**res**so
   (m.); *espresso with steamed milk*   il cappu**cci**no
(a) cold   il raffredd**o**re
colleague   il/la col**le**ga
commitment   l'imp**eg**no (m.)
connection   la coincid**en**za
contract   il contr**a**tto
cooked   c**o**tto, -a
cost: it costs   **co**sta
cough drops   le g**o**cce
credit card   la c**a**rta di cr**e**dito
cuttlefish   le s**e**ppie (pl.)

D

day   il gi**or**no; *per day*   al gi**o**rno
delicatessen   la salumer**i**a
delay   il rit**a**rdo; *late*   in rit**a**rdo; *I'm late*   s**o**no in ritardo
departure   la part**en**za
dessert   il d**o**lce
destination   la destinazi**o**ne
diarrhea   la diarr**e**a

director   il direttore
dish   il piatto; *typical (regional) dish*   la specialità; *dishes of the
   day*   I piatti del giorno
document   il documento
dollar   il dollaro
don't mention it   prego
to drink   bere; *something to drink*   qualcosa da bere
driving license   la patente
duck   l'anitra (f.)

E

to eat   mangiare
employee   l'impiegato (m.)
England   l'Inghilterra (f.)
enough   basta; *is that enough? is that all?*   basta così?
evening   la sera
excellent   buonissimo, -a, ottimo, -a
exchange   il cambio
excuse me   scusi
excuse me, may I pass through/come in?   permesso
expensive   caro, -a
express train   il rapido

F

fillet   il filetto
to find   trovare
(the) first   il primo; *the first course*   il primo (piatto); *the first
   floor*   il primo piano
fish   il pesce
flavor   il gusto
floor   il piano; *first floor*   il primo piano
for, to   per; *for me*   per me
free   libero, -a
French   francese (m. and f.)
fried   fritto, -a

from da
fruit la frutta
fruit vendor il fruttivendolo
fully booked al completo

G

garlic l'aglio (m.)
gas la benzina
gentleman il signore
German tedesco, -a
girl la ragazza
glass il bicchiere
to go andare; *go* (polite) vada; *go straight ahead* vada dritto;
   the way to. . . ? per andare a . . . ?
good buono, -a
goodbye arrivederci
goodnight buonanotte
grapefruit il pompelmo
Great Britain la Gran Bretagna
green verde

H

half mezzo; *a half kilo* un mezzo chilo
ham il prosciutto; *cured ham* il prosciutto crudo
handbag la borsetta
have: I have ho; *he/she has* ha, *you have* (polite), ha, *we
   have* abbiamo; *do you have any cheese?* ha del formaggio?
hello, good evening buonasera
hello, good morning buongiorno
hello, hi, bye ciao; *hello (on the phone)* pronto?
here qui; *here is . . .* ecco; *here is the coffee* ecco il caffè; *here
   they are* èccoli
historic storico, -a
holiday le ferie: *holiday closing* chiuso per ferie
hostel l'ostello (m.); *youth hostel* l'ostello della gioventù

hotel l'al**ber**go; *hotel manager* l'albergat**o**re (m.), l'albergat**ri**ce (f.); *small hotel* la pensi**o**ne: *with half-board* m**e**zza pensi**o**ne; *with full board* pensi**o**ne compl**e**ta

hour, time **o**ra: *at what time?* a che **o**ra?; *what time is it?* che **o**re s**o**no

how are you? (polite) c**o**me st**a**?

how do you do? piac**e**re

how many? qu**a**nti?

how much? qu**a**nto?; *how much does it cost?* qu**a**nto c**o**sta?; *how much is it?* quant'**è**?; *how much does it come to?* qu**a**nto viene?

(a) hundred grams etto

husband il ma**ri**to

I

I **i**o

I am s**o**no

I'll have pr**e**ndo; *they'll have* pr**e**ndono

I'm sorry dispi**a**ce, mi dispi**a**ce

I would like vorr**e**i

information le informazi**o**ni (pl.); *tourist information* le informazi**o**ni turistiche

ice cream il gel**a**to

immediately s**u**bito

in in

included incl**u**so; *everything included* t**u**tto incl**u**so

instead inv**e**ce

introduce: (may) I introduce my colleague? le pres**e**nto la m**i**a coll**e**ga?

Irish irland**e**se (m. and f.)

Italian itali**a**no, -a

K
---

key la chi**a**ve

kilo il chilo

kind gent**i**le; *you are very kind* (polite) **è** m**o**lto gent**i**le

L

lead   il pi**o**mbo; *lead-free*   s**e**nza pi**o**mbo
leather-goods shop   la valiger**i**a
leave: it leaves   **p**arte; *at what time does it leave?*   a che ora
   parte?
left   sin**i**stra; *to the left*   a sin**i**stra
lemon   il lim**o**ne
lemonade   la limon**a**ta
less   m**e**no
letter   la l**e**ttera
lift   l'ascen**so**re (m.)
lights (traffic)   il se**ma**foro; *at the lights*   al se**ma**foro
like: I like   mi pi**a**ce; *do you like it?* (polite)   le pi**a**ce?
like   c**o**me
lira   la l**i**ra
(a) little   po', un po'; *a little of*   un po' di . . .
lunch, main meal   il pr**a**nzo

M

managing director   il dirett**o**re
map   la pi**a**nta
market   il merc**a**to; *supermarket*   il supermerc**a**to
marketing director   il dirett**o**re delle v**e**ndite
matter: it does not matter   non im**po**rta
maximum   m**a**ssimo; *for a maximum of*   al m**a**ssimo di
may I help you (polite)?   de**si**dera?
me   me; *for me*   per me
me, to me   mi
meat   la c**a**rne
melon   il mel**o**ne
menu   il men**ù**
midday   mezzogi**o**rno
midnight   mezzan**o**tte
milk   il l**a**tte; *with milk*   al l**a**tte

Miss, young lady la signorina
mixed misto, -a
Monday il lunedì
more, plus più
(this) morning stamattina
Mr., sir il signor
Mrs., lady la signora
mushrooms funghi

N

name il nome; *what is your name?* (polite) come si chiama?
near vicino, -a
need: I need your passports mi servono i passaporti
next prossimo, -a
night la notte
no no
not non
nothing, no niente; *no dessert, thank you* niente dolce,
  grazie
now then allora
number il numero; *(room) number eleven* il numero undici;
  will you leave me your number? mi lascia il suo numero?

O

of di
office l'ufficio (m.); *in the office* in ufficio; *post office* l'ufficio
  postale; *main/head office* la sede
oil (olive) l'olio (m.); *with olive oil* all'olio
one-way (trip) andata
onion la cipolla
only soltanto
open aperto, -a
or oppure
orangeade l'aranciata (f.)
oranges arance

out, outside fuori; *outside the station* fuori della stazione
outlet (electrical) la presa di corrente
oven il forno; *oven-heated* al forno
owner (of a firm) il/la titolare

P

package, parcel il pacchetto
parmesan cheese il parmigiano
passport il passaporto
pasta, cake la pasta
patisserie la pasticceria
peach la pesca
perfume shop la profumeria
person la persona
pharmacy la farmacia
phone card la carta telefonica
piece il pezzo; *a piece of cheese* un pezzo di formaggio
pizza la pizza; *pizza with tomato sauce and mozzarella cheese* la
  pizza margherita
pizzeria la pizzeria
place, room il posto; *is there room?* c'è posto?
platform il binario; *from platform (four)* dal binario
  (quattro)
please per cortesia, per favore; *please go to, please sit down*
  accomodi, s'accomodi
pork il maiale
postcard la cartolina
pound sterling la sterlina
prefer: I prefer preferisco
price il prezzo

Q

quail la quaglia
(a) quarter quarto; un quarto; *a quarter past two* le due e un
  quarto

R

railway station   la stazione
raw; cured   crudo, -a; *cured ham*   prosciutto crudo
red   rosso, -a
rented   noleggiato; *I have rented*   ho noleggiato
to repeat   ripetere
reservation   la prenotazione
reserve: I have reserved   ho prenotato
restaurant   il ristorante; *small family restaurant*   la trattoria
return   il ritorno
rice   il riso
right   destra; *to the right*   a destra; *on the right*   sulla destra
risotto   il risotto
road   la strada
roll (bread)   il panino
(a) room with a double bed   matrimoniale; *a twin-bedded room*
   una camera a due letti
room service   il servizio in camera; *wake-up service*   il servizio
   sveglia
round-trip   andata e ritorno

S

salad   l'insalata (f.)
salmon   il salmone
sauce   la salsa
savory, salty   salato, -a
schedule/timetable   l'orario (m.)
Scottish   scozzese (m. and f.)
seasons   le stagioni
second course   il secondo
secretary   la segretaria
self-service restaurant   la tavola calda
shade   l'ombra; *in the shade*   all'ombra
shopkeeper   il/la negoziante

shower   la doccia
to sign   firmare; *can you (polite) sign?*   può firmare?
single   singola
small, little   piccolo, –a
smoking or non-smoking?   fumatori o non fumatori?
something   qualcosa; *something to drink*   qualcosa da bere
sorry: I'm sorry   mi dispiace
soup   la zuppa
to speak   parlare
spicy   piccante
stamp   il francobollo
station (railway)   la stazione
steak   la bistecca
stomachache   mal di stomaco
straight ahead   dritto; sempre dritto
strawberry   la fragola
string beans   i fagiolini
sugar   lo zucchero
Sunday   domenica
supermarket   il supermercato
supplement   il supplemento
swimming pool   la piscina

T

take-out establishment specializing in roast meats   la rosticceria
tea   il tè; *with lemon*   al limone
telephone   il telefono
telephone line   la linea; *hold the line*   rimanga in linea
telephone token   il gettone
television, TV set   la televisione
temporarily   temporaneamente
tent   la tenda
thank you   grazie; *that's all, thanks*   basta, grazie
then   quindi
then, anything else?   poi?

there là; *there is* c'**è**
this, this one qu**e**sto, -a
(a) thousand **mi**lle
thousand(s) **mi**la
thruway l'autost**ra**da (f.)
Thursday il giove**dì**
ticket il bigli**e**tto
ticket office la biglietter**i**a
tip la m**an**cia
tobacconist il tabacc**a**io
today **o**ggi
tomato il pomod**o**ro; *with tomato* al pomod**o**ro
tomorrow dom**a**ni; *the day after tomorrow* dopod**o**mani
too, too much tr**o**ppo
toothache mal di d**e**nti
toward v**e**rso; *at around three o'clock* v**e**rso le tr**e**
town la citt**à**
trade fair la fi**e**ra
train (express) il r**a**pido; *train stopping at all stations* il loc**a**le
trip il vi**a**ggio
trout la tr**o**ta
Tuesday il marte**dì**
tuna fish il tonno; *with tuna fish sauce* al t**on**no
turn g**i**ri (polite); *turn left* g**i**ri a sin**i**stra
twin-bedded room d**o**ppia, camera d**o**ppia
type il t**i**po
typical of a region region**a**le

U

understand: I didn't understand non ho cap**i**to
until **fi**no

V

VAT excluded IVA escl**u**sa
veal il vit**e**llo

vegetable, salad dish   il contorno
vegetables   la verdura
vegetarian   vegetariano, -a
very   molto

W

wallet   il portafoglio
water   l'acqua (f.); *mineral water*   l'acqua minerale; *sparkling
   mineral water*   l'acqua minerale gassata (or frizzante); *regular
   mineral water*   l'acqua minerale non gassata (or naturale)
we, us   noi
we are   siamo
well   bene; *OK, fine*   va bene; *very well, very good*   benissimo
Welsh   gallese (m. and f.)
what   cosa; *what will you have?*   cosa prendono?
what is (it)?   cos'è?
when?   quando?
where?   dove? *where is?*   dov'è?
which one?   quale?
white   bianco, -a
who?   chi? *who shall I say?*   chi devo dire?
wine   il vino; *your house wine*   il vostro vino della casa
wine shop   la cantina
with   con
without   senza
would you like?   (polite) vuole?

Y

yes   sì
yesterday   ieri

NOTES

N O T E S

NOTES